with the
Devil

AUDREY HARPER

with Harry Pugh

KINGSWAY PUBLICATIONS

EASTBOURNE

Front cover design by Vic Mitchell

British Library Cataloguing in Publication Data

Harper, Audrey
 Dance with the Devil : a young woman's struggle to escape
 the coven's curse.
 1. Witches – Biographies
 I. Title   II. Pugh, Harry
 133.43092

 ISBN 0–86065–850–3

Printed in Great Britain for
KINGSWAY PUBLICATIONS LTD
1 St Anne's Road, Eastbourne, E Sussex BN21 3UN by
Courier International Ltd, Tiptree, Essex
Typeset by Watermark, Norfolk House, Cromer NR27 9HL

Contents

HARRY PUGH was for 27 years a reporter with the Express Newspaper group. Among his recent assignments were major investigations into aspects of the occult, including witchcraft. He is now a freelance journalist based in Herefordshire.

Foreword

Dance with the Devil is one of the most important books on the evils of devil worship published for many years.

Sad to report, Audrey's story is not untypical, because the fear of the devil put into victims makes them too terrified to tell and break away. Audrey Harper has bravely escaped from the terrors of satanism and black witchcraft. I am delighted that, with the support of Christ, Audrey Harper has found the strength to tell her story through the pen of Harry Pugh.

Such was my concern about the spread of devil worship, and the abuse of children during their rituals, that I warned Parliament. The publicity given to my debate brought forth new information and many convictions have followed. More recently, the NSPCC have issued a report confirming the growth of the occult and the child abuse element, and I am constantly monitoring court cases.

We shall beat these evil minded people – but only if we fight spiritual fire with fire.

God bless you, Audrey Harper, and keep you safe.

GEOFFREY DICKENS JP MP
Child Protection Campaigner

Important Note

In this factual account it has been necessary to include reports of satanic rites and practices which, while essential to the story, may be upsetting to some readers.

1

A Strange Case

Why the devil should choose me to be his dancing partner, I will never know. It's a question I have asked myself time and time again.

Was I born to serve Satan? Did I have some genetic quality that appealed to him? Did he pick me out when I was a mischievous teenager? Was there something in my loveless upbringing that singled me out? Or was it some kind of cruel accident that I fell into his clutches?

Lots of questions, and no answers. But the truth remains—I served Satan as a loyal and willing member of a black magic coven, and kept my secret for twenty-five years.

I often wanted to tell, but didn't dare. In the early stages, I was afraid for myself. Later, I was afraid for my family. And all the time I was afraid people simply wouldn't believe me. When I did finally tell what I had seen, it was to an audience of millions watching a TV show.

Judging by the response, my few, carefully chosen words had quite an impact. The press were knocking at my door and my name was in the headlines. I didn't want publicity. I didn't seek sensationalism. But I suppose it's not every day that somebody goes before the cameras and reveals that she has witnessed the murder of a baby in a witchcraft ceremony, as well as organised child

11

abuse parties for the purposes of pornography to finance the coven.

I had been carrying the awful secret far too long. It had haunted my sleep and almost driven me crazy with worry. Now I was glad it was out in the open. It was not a pretty story, as you will soon discover, but it had to be told.

But there was a shock in store. One morning soon after the TV show a young policeman arrived at my door. The police from Virginia Water in Surrey (where the coven had been based) had been in touch with the local station. My story, it seemed, had got back to source and they were sending two officers to investigate it. Would I see them?

I was flabbergasted. More than twenty-five years after I had seen a murder being committed, the police were at last going to investigate it.

In one way I was pleased. If the coven at Virginia Water was still active, police action might stop it. They might even be able to arrest and charge the evil members with some of their crimes.

But looking at it from another viewpoint, I was extremely worried. Would they arrest me? After all, I had committed a serious offence—I had seen a baby being murdered and done nothing about it.

I agreed to see the officers. What else could I do? But first I went to a solicitor, and I made sure he was a Christian solicitor, recommended by the Evangelical Alliance, who at least would believe in the power of Satan and give my story some credence.

The solicitor, Andrew Keen from Birmingham, admitted he was worried after I told him what I had seen. Worried—for my sake. It incriminated me, and made me an accessory. But we decided that I should go ahead and tell the whole story to the police.

Two officers, Det Supt Rose and Det Inspector Amos,

travelled to Birmingham to question me, and I spent five hours with them in Ladywood Police Station going over my life story.

They wanted to know everything about me, almost as much as I'm telling in this book. As well as what happened to me during the years when I was a witch, they asked me about my upbringing, my activities as a prostitute, my life as a junkie—everything. In all, my statement ran to nine closely-written foolscap pages.

I kept nothing back. There was no point. Parts of the story I told several times over as they prodded and prised to test the truth of it. But after the gap of time there was no way of proving it. It was simply my word which I laid before them as truthfully as memory would allow.

Before we started Supt Rose said to me: 'Are you sure you don't want to back out and retract this story?'

'No,' I said. 'Why should I?'

'If you're not telling the truth we'll find out, and you could be prosecuted for wasting police time.'

'My story is absolutely true,' I told him. 'I'd love it not to be, but it is.'

There were times during the five hours when I just had to stop, especially when I was describing the scenes of child abuse I had witnessed. What had happened to me was bad enough, but I felt so upset at having to go through some of the dreadful things I had witnessed, I broke down and cried.

The police officers were patient, understanding and extremely courteous. But whether they believed my story I cannot say. Unless you believe in the power of Satan, it's difficult to conceive that his followers are capable of such horrific deeds.

It must be especially difficult for policemen, schooled to deal in hard facts, to investigate occult matters where strange things occur without any earthly explanation. I could not give them names and addresses, times and dates, phone numbers and car registrations—the nitty-gritty details needed for a successful police investigation. I did my best to describe the people and places in Virginia Water who were involved in the coven, but after twenty-five years my memory was hazy and I don't think I was much help.

At the end of the session, the superintendent said: 'You have now done what you should have done twenty-five years ago—reported this to us. But it can't be changed. Put it behind you and carry on with the good work you're doing.'

With hindsight, I know I should have reported that dreadful crime at the time. But I was terrified—and with Satan breathing down my neck, I thought I would be struck down before I reached a police station. Police protection is not much of a shield to a threat from Satan.

The police went away saying they would carry on with the investigation. I doubt if they will ever get anywhere. But my story, even if it cannot be taken further at the moment, may have achieved something.

Next time a child is reported missing, or next time the body of a baby is found, the police might look towards witchcraft as a possible cause.

It is my belief that witchcraft is flourishing today as widely as ever it was in the Middle Ages. We see evidence in the courts of child abuse and other evils that are the work of Satan. Fortunately, I am not alone in this belief. Many other people—clergymen, politicians, social workers—are alert to the dangers.

Why Satan chose me I shall never know. But I do know one thing. Once the devil has taken you as his dancing partner, he hates to let you go.

2

Home Away from Home

The story I told the police officers had begun nearly fifty years earlier when a tiny baby, born on Christmas Day in 1939 just a few months after the start of the Second World War, was handed over to be brought up by the nurses at a Dr Barnardo's Home.

I grew to resent my mother, perhaps unfairly, for not showing me the love and care a parent should. If she had had more money, I might have had a normal family upbringing, and none of those terrible things that were to blight my later years would have happened.

But my father had died—I still don't know how—three months before I was born, leaving her with four older children to bring up. The new baby was just too much. It would have to go.

My sister Pauline, who is just a couple of years older, was also packed off to Dr Barnardo's from the two-roomed flat behind an optician's shop in Crewe where my mother tried to run the family home. Pauline returned home after a few years. But not me. I never rejoined my family.

The home was called Farm Hill in the Essex village of Kelvedon, famous for its sweet peas. There were fields and fields of them and, while they were blossoming in the summer, the smell used to waft through the countryside. Even now, whenever I smell sweet peas, I think of that place.

When I was very young, I wasn't conscious of missing family life. I suppose those feelings started when I was six or seven. By that time I was out of the kindergarten and in the main part of the home.

They divided us into houses by giving each age group a name. The youngest, at five when we had started school, were Imps. Those in the group a year older were Pixies. The next group up were Elves.

It would have been when I was either a Pixie or an Elf that I began to realise that I was missing out on something. Groups of people used to visit the home regularly, and the children would sing for them, and serve them tea and cakes. Always after these visits some of my friends would disappear.

It was a little while before I discovered what was happening. These groups of nice people were coming to view with the intention of adopting a child. So that was where my friends were going—to wealthy homes where they would have a lovely life with all their own things.

But I was never chosen, and much later I found out why. It wasn't because I was ugly or unpleasant. It was simply because my mother had hoped that one day she would be able to afford to take me back home, so I wasn't marked down for adoption.

Not being able to have your own possessions was, I think, one of the worst aspects of life in that home. If you were given a toy, or a game for Christmas, it would be yours for a few days, then it would be sucked into the pool to be shared by everybody else. I wanted so desperately to have something I could call my own.

At holiday times we were put up by kind families in the locality. But there was one holiday when I was put on the train and sent to spend a couple of weeks with my mother in Crewe when I was about ten years old.

My mother seemed harassed and ill-tempered. She

sent me to buy a reel of cotton but shopping was something we were never given to do at the home. I couldn't find the shop, and I went back without the cotton. Mother shouted at me and called me stupid which I thought was unfair. That was the only time I ever went home for a holiday.

From the age of five, we went to school at Coggleshall, a walk of nearly three miles from the home. About twenty of us set off to walk there every morning in our navy blue raincoats and dark blue skirts. The other children used to call us the Banana Bunch—a corruption of Barnado's. In the summer the walk was pleasant enough. Sometimes we'd sneak into the fields and pick bunches of sweet peas to give to the teachers.

But it wasn't so nice in the winter. I remember walking through deep snow one bad winter. Our gloves were on a piece of elastic going up the sleeves of our coats. You had to be careful not to lose one, otherwise you would have cold hands all winter. The matron sewed up all the coat pockets. She didn't like to see the Banana Bunch with their hands in their pockets.

It was a harsh regime, and the matron, whom I nicknamed the Witch, could be spiteful. She was a severe-looking lady with greying hair. I was terrified of her, and used to have vivid nightmares of her riding a broomstick. If we did anything wrong, her favourite punishment was to rap us over the knuckles with a hairbrush. She used to do this with all the other children standing around to witness your misfortune. And it was extremely painful. On one occasion she managed to break a bone in one of the boy's hands.

With all the hundreds of boys and girls who passed through the home, I suppose she had to be a disciplinarian. Some of us must have been little terrors. I was one of them.

But she could be kind, and on Mother's Day we used

to make little posies for her with flowers we picked in the hedgerows. We managed to have a lot of fun in spite of the discipline.

There was a donkey we used to play with, and a pony called Tiny. One of the nurses sometimes came to meet us from school with the donkey trap. Getting it to move, though, was something else. Invariably we'd finish up pulling the donkey back.

I'll never forget the day Tiny arrived. He was a bad-tempered little thing and nobody could ride him. But my friend Tina and I, the daredevils, were determined not to be beaten by a moody nag.

It took us half-an-hour to catch him. Tina held his mane while I climbed on using a chair from the dining room. I think I stayed on for four paces before he sent me flying. I wasn't hurt, but the chair was smashed to bits, and the matron was none too pleased about that.

We soon found a way of avoiding trouble. We would make nests in the long grass for when any of the staff came looking for us. I've seen large groups vanish in that meadow by going to ground at the sound of the matron's bark.

When I felt annoyed, the piano was a great release. Tina also played. We would strum out duets together. It was amazing how hammering out a jolly little melody could make you forget your troubles.

Each of the groups had their own dormitory with perhaps eight or nine beds. But there was no individual wardrobe or cupboard space. You were not allowed to build up your own little store of possessions, things you could call your own.

I remember being given a little gold cross by the music teacher at school for doing well at piano playing. I took it home and put it by a window in the dormitory. The following morning it had gone.

My prayer book also vanished. I was given it at the

age of twelve when I was confirmed at the local church. It had my name inscribed and I was very proud of it. But I only had it three days before the matron confiscated it as a punishment after I had wet my bed. I never saw that prayer book again.

I liked going to school, largely because it got me out of the home. But I was quite good as well, in the primary school, at subjects like spelling and writing and painting. Generally I was classed as a bright pupil, but I was mischievous and for ever getting the cane.

The cane at school was nothing—just a tickle with a ruler across the hands. But you had to swear the other kids to secrecy. If matron found out you had been punished at school, she would give you a second punishment—her raps with the hairbrush.

Her favourite punishment was the cellar-cleaning sentence. There were three big cellars where they kept stores of vegetables and other food. They had cement floors, and you had to get down on your knees and scrub them. If your offence had been really bad, you would be locked in the cellar shivering all night, with only the sound of the rats scuttling about for company. I was kept down there once for most of the night for not cleaning the younger children's shoes properly.

As well as our school work, we had to work hard at the home. There were jobs first thing in the morning before we went to school. And there were others when we got home. As you got older, the tasks got harder. I found myself washing and putting the younger children to bed, and then washing their clothes and darning their socks so they would be spick and span to go to school the next morning.

Looking after the tiny ones was something I enjoyed. There was always a lot of joking and laughing at bedtime when I read them stories. I used to get as much fun out of it as they did.

The routine at the home was a bit like the forces. Each of the bedrooms had a brown linoleum floor which had to be polished every morning until it was gleaming. The matron would then go round on a tour of inspection and if she found a speck of dust there would be trouble. All of this had to be done before you could have your breakfast. Sometimes it was just too much and it made me late for school.

We were never given any pocket money. Interestingly, this encouraged dishonesty. I remember going around the pockets of children's coats in the school cloakroom and stealing a few pennies to spend on sweets at the shop.

There was still rationing in those days, but the kindly woman who ran the village stores would always let the Banana Bunch, distinctive in our red blouses and blue skirts, have a few liquorice allsorts, or sherbert dips, without coupons.

I found another way round the pocket money shortage. On Sundays we went to church. The younger children had to go twice, but as we got older we were marched off three times. I didn't enjoy it—it was too regimented. While learning the Ten Commandments, we were breaking one of them. The early grounding in my later career as a thief came at those compulsory church services. I became adept at slipping a coin or two from the collection plate into my pocket. If we had been given pocket money, I don't think I would have done it.

I was doing quite well at school. I was the only child in my group to pass the entrance examination to a grammar school. It meant I was parted from my pals, but I loved being away from the home.

At the new school at Colchester, I soon made friends. I've always had a capacity for making friends easily. I was popular in the class because I was mischievous and would do things to upset the teachers that the other girls were afraid to do. It made me a bit of a heroine.

Many of my classmates came to school on their bicycles; I was so envious as they arrived on their gleaming machines. I'd never even ridden a bike. But a plot soon formed in my mind—one that would result in my first brush with the law.

Some of the nurses at the home had bicycles which they kept in a shed in the grounds. My plan was a daring one, and I knew it would get me into big trouble. But I had to experience the feeling of riding a bike to school.

I got up early, and took the best bike in the shed. It had a three-speed and drop handle-bars. I wobbled a bit when I took off, but I soon had it mastered, and I cycled the fifteen miles to school, feeling free as a bird. It was a glorious feeling with the wind in my hair. I was like somebody who had been just let out of jail. I knew I would be late for school but I didn't care. I was a girl with a bike, not a deprived kid from the home. I felt really proud, telling my friends it was a present.

After school, I had to cycle back to the home. Out in the traffic, my confidence was growing. But I must have done something wrong to the three-speed and messed up the gears. Suddenly I found nothing was happening though I was pedalling like mad. It broke down near the home of one of my friends so I pushed it into her garden and hid it. Then I got on the bus and went back to the home.

It was not until the following morning that the nurse missed her bike. There was a bit of a hue and cry but I kept my mouth shut. The police were informed and they must have made inquiries at the school because the bike was found in my friend's shed—and then, of course, I was caught.

The police sergeant questioned me at the home, and

I told him I had taken it. He was marvellous—and I think he realised that we kids didn't have very much, and understood my need to have that bike for a day. I remember telling him how much I'd love a bike, but as we didn't get any pocket money, I couldn't save up to buy one.

I expected the Matron to give me the works. If she could break a boy's knuckle for bed wetting, what sort of a punishment would she think fit for bike stealing? But the bashing I expected never materialised. I think the police sergeant must have had a quiet word with her. I got a telling off, and that was all.

It was about this time the great escape plot was hatched. There was no one specific cause—I talked it over with a girl called Alice, and as we both hated life at the home, it seemed a good idea.

We made our plans like those prisoners at Colditz. I sneaked into the cellar, and filled two paper bags with oranges and bananas and made off through the front door. We should have gone to bed, but we went out into the darkness.

We didn't get very far—just a couple of miles to the village of Kelvedon. It was a cold October night, and we were both shivering. Alice started crying and said she wanted to go back. She was sitting on a seat in the middle of the village just waiting to be picked up.

We were missed before long, and the matron and one of the nurses came out in a car looking for us. They soon found Alice, but I had hidden in a field. I didn't want to go back. But the police then joined in the hunt and Alice told them where I was hiding, so they picked me up and took me to the police station.

It was the same sergeant who had been so nice about the stolen bike. I was very tearful, and I told him I would be in awful trouble and didn't want to go back. He took me back to the home, and the matron locked me in the cellar in the dark for the rest of the night.

It was freezing cold, and I was scared. I'm sure she would have kept me there all the next day as well, if the sergeant hadn't come to the home and said he wanted to talk to me. The matron could switch on the charm when anybody in authority came to the home.

It wasn't my last escape bid. Altogether, I ran away about half-a-dozen times. Once I got as far as Colchester by hitching a lift. But I was never away for long. It didn't take the police long to spot a teenager in school uniform with a scarlet beret walking along roads at night, and they soon had me back under the spell of the Witch.

Even though I had a lot of pals at school, I used to get terribly lonely. There were one or two girls who used to invite me to their homes, but I could never develop these friendships, because we were never allowed to invite friends back to the home.

I often used to think how lovely it would be if I lived with a family and could have my friends round for meals or to play music or watch television. But there were none of these things in my life.

This loneliness, more than anything, was the cause of my developing a bad record at school. I used to do things the other girls would be afraid to do, just to draw attention to myself.

The history mistress was a bit of an old ditherer, and I once put glue on her chair. She never found out who had done it, but all the girls knew. This bravado made me popular, but it didn't bring me friends, true friends, the close relationships I so badly wanted.

In spite of my reluctance to work, I got five O-levels when I sat my exams. Not a bad little bunch of qualifications for someone who hadn't bothered to swot, but the school made it quite plain they didn't want me to stay on. They were fed up with my behaviour, and told matron so.

At sixteen, you finish at Dr Barnardo's Homes, and I was very glad when my sixteenth birthday came. At last I would be away! The matron found me a job as a children's nurse at a home in Chelmsford but it was a few months before I could start, and she kept me working at Farm Hill, looking after the tiny tots there.

There was a minor scandal in the home when one of the girls, Jean, had a baby. I thought the matron was going to have apoplexy when she heard about it. Poor Jean. After that, her life was a misery. She was given all the dirty jobs to do, and she was never allowed out.

One day Jean said to me: 'There's a Youth for Christ meeting in Colchester. Will you come with me?'

Yes, I said. I'd go along. Jean was so out of favour I didn't think she would be permitted to go, but as it was a religious occasion, the matron agreed, and off we went.

But we weren't going to a Youth for Christ meeting at all. Jean had arranged dates with a couple of soldiers in the town and we went to the flicks with them. That became a monthly event—meeting our soldiers on the pretence of going to religious meetings.

The matron was quite a religious lady. There was a little chapel in the home. But at that time of my life, I wasn't terribly interested. My prime interests were clothes and money, and I didn't have any of either.

When I started at Chelmsford, I worked hard and enthusiastically. I was used to looking after babies, having had plenty of experience at the Dr Barnardo nursery. So it wasn't surprising that I got my qualifications—Nursery Nurse Exam Board—in one year instead of the usual two. I'll never forget picking up my first month's wages. How much it was I can't remember, but I went out and blew the lot on clothes. I bought a couple of flared skirts and blouses and jumpers, and some nice underwear instead of the old things I had been given at Farm Hill. I bought shoes and a pretty nightdress. After a couple of hours I hadn't got a penny left, but I felt good with my new wardrobe.

Having money and nice new clothes were two new experiences. But they did not make up for the lack of love. With love, my life might have turned out differently—and Satan might have been denied a recruit.

But soon I was to be a recruit of a different kind. Shortly after passing my exams I took a trip to London. Near Liverpool Street Station was a recruiting office for the Woman's Royal Air Force.

The posters looked interesting—and it would be a chance to meet new people, make new friends and see new places. Without hesitation, I walked in and signed on.

3

Twice Loved and Lost

I enjoyed my time in the Women's Royal Air Force. It was an impulse that made me walk into that recruiting office and sign on but, looking back, I feel there must have been some deeper motivation than the smart uniform, and those posters showing far-away lands with their promise of travel and adventure.

I honestly believe I was searching for the home and family I never had. Sometimes I found myself yearning for family life—for parents and brothers and sisters and relatives I could talk to, share confidences with, seek advice from. But I had nobody.

In Doctor Barnardo's you make friends, but at sixteen all of you are dispersed so you don't see each other any more. These homes have many good points, but nothing can take the place of a loving family upbringing.

At the time that I went into the WRAF, I was a bright eighteen-year-old, healthy, used to hard work, not terribly religious, used to discipline, and a virgin. Some of the girls may have fallen during their later years at Farm Hill. But I hadn't. I had never even seen a naked male, let alone been to bed with one.

After signing on for four years, I was sent to Wilmslow in Cheshire for my square-bashing and I became LAC 2831480 Wilbraham. Some of the girls found the training tough going, but I was used to the regimentation—the handing out of clothes, cutlery, and the kit inspections. It wasn't so different from life in the Banana Bunch.

In the barracks we were sleeping eight to a billet. We were only there for six weeks so there wasn't really time to make close chums. Some of the girls were a bit weepy. It was the first time they had been separated from their parents, and they were missing home sweet home. But it didn't affect me.

Many of the things we had to do I was already used to. Making beds, for instance. I'd been making my own bed since I could stand up. But some of the girls had always had their beds made by Mum and didn't know how it was done. And buffing up our shoes—I was an expert. As well as doing my own, I was showing the other girls how.

I loved my square-bashing. The only time I had any pangs was when it finished. All the other girls had parents and families there to watch the passing out parade. I had nobody.

But everything else was great. I liked the marching, the discipline, and I could even put up with the shouting of the NCOs. They always shout at recruits, but I had been shouted at and given orders all my life. Nothing was different.

I also liked the money. I made arrangements to have half my pay put into a Post Office savings account. For the first time in my life I had as much money as I needed—and extra to save. The only items I used money for were a bit of make-up and toothpaste and perhaps a night at the flicks. All my clothes and food were provided. I felt like Rothschild.

After passing out, I had to decide which career to follow in the forces. It came down to two choices—music or nursing. I had learned to play the piano and the violin at Farm Hill but I thought nursing had more prospects. So I put my name down, and was posted to do a basic medical course, and after that finished up at the RAF hospital at

Halton in Buckinghamshire. We were nursing military personnel, but the training and shiftwork were just like at any other hospital. I was studying for my State Registered Nurse examinations.

It was at Halton that I met David, my first boyfriend. He was a national serviceman. He came from a wealthy family who owned a string of TV shops in London.

He had bought me a drink one night in the NAAFI. Most of the guys would buy you a drink expecting you to go to bed with them. David was different. We enjoyed talking to each other. He was a keen photographer and he said he would like to take some pictures of me.

He took pictures of me in the fields and woods around the camp. It was sweet and innocent. He knew I was lonely. We were just jolly good pals who enjoyed each other's company.

After three months or so of this idyllic friendship, things began to get serious. He told me he was falling in love with me, and I told him I loved him too.

Then he shocked me by saying: 'If you love me, you should come to bed with me.'

I was flabbergasted. I said to him: 'If you loved me, you wouldn't ask me to do things I've never done before.'

We had an awful row about it. He had a little sports car, and I remember a long journey in total silence. I didn't sleep with him then, but I believe we were in love and, within a couple of months, we were sleeping together.

He took me for a weekend leave to London to meet his parents. They lived in a swish house. These fine surroundings emphasised our completely different backgrounds. But David swore that he loved me, and his parents accepted me.

That weekend he bought me a ring. He hadn't asked me to marry him, but it was an expensive diamond ring. I was thrilled. But on the way back to the camp, he broke the bad news—he was being posted abroad to Bahrein.

My soaring happiness turned to tears. But in my heart I knew that this sort of separation was to be expected in the forces. If you get a posting, you don't argue—you go. I was to lose him—all I could do was hope that it would not be for too long.

David had completed eighteen months of his two years' National Service when he was posted. I consoled myself that he would be back in six months, and then we could get married. We were writing to each other almost every day. It was then I discovered I was pregnant.

At first I didn't want to believe it. Life seemed so full of promise I didn't want anything to happen that could spoil it. For a while, I didn't tell anyone. Then I mustered up the courage to write to David and tell him I was carrying his child.

I needn't have worried. He was quite excited at the idea of becoming a father. He wrote back saying he would get home as quickly as he could. So I settled down to await him.

He never arrived. It was his mother who told me why. His plane had crashed shortly after take-off—he had died in the desert. She broke the news to me as gently as she could, but I reeled away from that telephone with the feeling that, just like that plane in the desert, my world had come crashing down.

This was the first person I'd loved, and now I'd lost him. The promise of a happy life as a wife and mother had been wiped out. David's parents didn't even know about the unborn child. I had nobody to turn to, no one to share my grief. So I turned to the bottle.

Until I joined the WRAF, I had never even tasted alcohol. During all those years at Dr Barnardo's, not even a sip of wine had passed my lips. But now, my head hurting with grief, I went on my first bender, and got absolutely legless.

How I got into bed I do not know. But the following morning the girls who shared my billet couldn't wake me up. I was so ill from the effects of the drink they admitted me to a hospital bed in the very ward where I had been working—the psychiatric ward.

I lay in that bed day after day mulling over my sorry state. With David dead, I didn't want the baby. But I had gone past the time for an abortion. I think the reason I didn't want it was that I knew I would get kicked out of the WRAF. I loved my life in the services, but they wouldn't want me with a baby. I was advised by the doctors that the best thing I could do was have a medical discharge. This would leave the way open for me to return after the baby was born.

I stayed in until I was six months pregnant, then the RAF arranged accommodation for me in a home in London for unmarried mothers. I had to pay the bills myself out of my savings. It was a pleasant enough place but I didn't want to be there. I wanted to be doing my job—nursing in the RAF Hospital.

One afternoon I decided to contact David's parents. I rang them up and they asked me to call and see them. I told them then that I was carrying their son's baby, and he was on his way home to marry me when he died in the crash.

I half hoped that they might invite me to stay with them, and have the baby there. That didn't happen, although they were very kind. They came to see me and took me out and gave me money to supplement my fast dwindling savings.

The baby was born in hospital, a little boy. I decided to call him Robin. David's parents came round to visit the hospital. When they saw it was a boy, they immediately offered to adopt him.

They were orthodox Jews, and a girl would not have

meant as much to them. But they wanted Robin. For some reason, at that time, I had a bit of a thing about the Jews, and I didn't want my baby brought up in the Jewish faith. So I refused.

They pleaded. 'If we bring him up, we can give him everything.'

But my mind was made up. 'No. I'm keeping him.'

I never saw David's family again. Once I had let them know they could not have the child, they were no longer interested in me. But I didn't care. I loved Robin. He was a happy child with great big bright eyes and light brown hair. He filled my life, and I was obsessed with him.

The rules of the home meant I was only allowed to stay for a month after Robin's birth. The matron helped me find lodgings with an elderly couple. But with no money, I had to find a job. I found work at a special home for young men suffering from muscular dystrophy.

So I would work in the day and spend the evenings fussing over my little boy. But things started going wrong when the elderly couple said they couldn't look after Robin, so I had to find somewhere else for him.

I found another couple who were prepared to look after him. They were lovely, and he was happy there. I used to go to see him in the evenings. He would be laying in his crib in front of the fire. But then I was told to leave my lodgings. Now I was homeless. The people who were looking after Robin persuaded me it would be kinder to let them adopt him, as he had got used to them and they had become very attached to him.

I don't know why, but I caved in. Perhaps it was the desperation of not being able to find anywhere to live. I agreed to let them adopt him, and I signed the necessary documents. I felt bitter at losing my son, but at the time it seemed the sensible thing to do. That was the last I saw of him.

Life was miserable without my little boy, but I soon discovered that misery can be suppressed with drink. I took to drinking fairly heavily, and went out with the girls most nights.

At that time I was living in a little flat. But I got the sack from my job in a vacuum cleaner factory, for getting drunk on duty, and with no money coming in to pay the rent, I soon had to give it up. With no home and no job, there were no roots to keep me in Brentwood. So I decided to go and have a look at the Big City.

I had about £150 in my pocket—the total of my life-savings. But if I thought this would get me accommodation in London, I was sadly wrong. I made some enquiries in the Victoria area, but everybody wanted payment for a month in advance, and key money as well. So I thought I'd wait a while, and I spent my first night sleeping at Victoria Coach Station.

That is how I became a drifter. I made for the place where all the other young drifters who go to London end up—sitting on the steps in the middle of Piccadilly Circus.

4

Eros in the City

The statue of Eros in Piccadilly Circus is at the hub of London. And at the start of the Swinging Sixties, it became the focal point of my life.

It was a fitting place for me to spend my days. For there are sinister aspects in the background of the Greek god of love. Eros, it seems, has a darker side to his character. The hare, the cockerel and the goat, all important symbols in witchcraft, are associated with him.

According to some ancient writers, Eros was the son of Chaos—and there has certainly been plenty of that in my life. Already, at the tender age of twenty-one, I had had my fair share of it.

The people who sat on those steps with London whirling around them had a different outlook from the rest of the world. They were oblivious to the milling crowds and thrumming traffic. I found it bewildering, and felt a little bit out of place. Most of my new neighbours were filthy, but at this stage my jeans, shirt and jacket—the only clothes I'd brought—were clean.

I eyed the people around me, wondering whether I should talk to them. I decided to let them talk to me first. I had quite a long wait. It must have been two hours before anybody said anything to me. Then a long-haired lad, whom I later found was called Jeff, shuffled a bit closer.

'Have you got anywhere to go?' he asked.

Later I discovered from Jeff and the two people with him that any newcomer on the steps is spotted instantly. And they have a way of recognising the homeless ones from tourists who just sit down for a rest.

He seemed a friendly young man. This was the era of flower power and he had a serene look on his face.

I replied to his question: 'No, I haven't. I've just moved up here. I'm looking for somewhere to live.'

He introduced me to the girl and the other man in the group. They all began to talk about accommodation problems.

Jeff said: 'It's possible to live in London without paying any rent, you know.'

I was interested. I didn't really want to blow my £150 on renting a flat or digs, not before I had a job anyway. They told me they were living in a derelict house in Balham and they said I could join them if I wished.

I was about to go and buy a packet of cigarettes, but Jeff said: 'No. Get them later. Have one of ours first.'

He took out what I thought was tobacco and two cigarette papers. He used both papers to roll up the mixture, making it twice as long as a normal cigarette, and carefully twisted the ends. It was a reefer, but I didn't yet realise that I was having my first taste of marijuana.

I guessed it was no ordinary cigarette when they began to pass it around. When I blew out the smoke, Jeff said: 'No. Don't waste it. Inhale it and keep it down.'

I did as I was told when the joint was next passed to me. The smoke tasted peculiar. Slowly, I began to float. It was as if I was the only person in the whole of Piccadilly. But I found I was enjoying the sensation.

I liked my new friends and I liked the strange cigarettes they passed around. I was the only one with any money so I bought them all supper. By this time the group had increased to six. I went to a shop and came back with six portions of fish and chips.

It was a warm July evening and we sat around until close to midnight. By now the happy crowd of hippies had been swollen by other people. They had grey sallow faces and didn't laugh. They were the serious addicts gathering to get their prescriptions of heroin at the all-night chemist.

The registered addicts were given doctor's prescriptions but the chemist would not hand over the drugs before the date the doctor had entered. So they would hang around until midnight. Then, when the new day was minutes old, they would troop into Boots to get their legal ration of heroin.

After that there was a great deal of activity. People were diving down to the toilets to prepare their syringes and pump the drug into their veins. Others were trading—selling half their prescribed dose to other addicts who were not registered. It was like a market place where everyone dealt in the same deadly commodity. Little did I know that within a few months I'd be among them, bargaining and bartering for a fix.

But that first night I didn't like the heroin addicts. I didn't trust them. I felt that if they knew I had money, they would try to take it from me. So I wandered off to an all-night café.

I hung around most of the night and then made my way back to Victoria. By this time I was feeling tired so I grabbed a few hours' sleep at the coach station. But in the morning I made my way back up to the Dilly, and round about the middle of the day Jeff and my other hippy friends had arrived.

Jeff had been to university but had dropped out. I never found out very much about the others. We never talked about where we came from or how we came to be there. Such things as background belonged to the past, and the past did not concern them. Nor the future. All they were concerned about was the present. They lived from one joint to the next, never planning, never worrying where the next meal was coming from. But they were a happy crowd.

Alas, I can't say the same for the people on the other side of the street. The public looked with disgust as they passed us step dwellers. We might have been a little drunk, or a little high, but we were harmless. Yet I was actually spat on by people who thought we were scum.

The second night, after sitting for hours in the Dilly smoking joints, eating chips and drinking vodka and lager, I accompanied my new friends to the squat in Balham. As well as showing me how to live rent-free, they taught me the tricks of free travel, or bilking as it's called.

We rode the Tube, but we rarely paid. One of the group would start complaining that a ticket machine was faulty and while the attention of the staff was occupied, the rest of us would nip through. When we got to Balham, we just jostled our way past the collector and ran for it.

The house where the nine-strong group was living had been condemned and was boarded up. But they had forced the backdoor, and were occupying a couple of the downstairs rooms. There were holes in the floorboards where they had rotted through, and other boards had been ripped to light a fire. The electricity had long been cut off, but in the flickering light of a candle I could see dirty mattresses spread around the floor.

The whole place was filthy and it stank. It was obvious that there were rats there. But it was a free home for the hippies. This was the hospitality my new friends offered me, a single mattress on the floor of this squalid place.

I was tired and I accepted gratefully, but the lingering stench in my nostrils stopped me having a proper night's sleep. I was mighty glad to get out in the morning and breathe the pure fresh air of Balham.

I was happy enough with the people, but I didn't want to go back to that unpleasant squat. So I spent my days with them hanging around the Dilly, and at night I did my own thing. There are plenty of places to sleep in London as long as it's not too cold. There are railway and coach stations. There are parks. And there are cardboard boxes in shop doorways, or under the arches by the Embankment. I slept in them all.

After a month or so of this drifting, I was shocked to find how much my money had dwindled. I wasn't spending anything on accommodation—and not a lot on food. A hot dog a day was my ration. Booze and cigarettes were gobbling up my savings, and I was a little too recklessly generous towards my friends who had nothing.

I couldn't get a job, and as I got dirtier, the chances of finding one diminished. Having no address meant I couldn't claim unemployment benefit, or social security money. If there was a way to get help from the State, I never found it.

But I did find a way of getting clean. And it was free. At Victoria Station there were public baths. They charged two shillings for soap, hot water and a towel, but I didn't have two shillings to spare. The woman in charge took pity on me.

'You need a bath,' she said. 'Have one on me.'

She was a lovely woman and we became good friends. Her name was Florence—I called her Flo. Every fortnight she would let me have a free bath and wash my hair and clothes, and I'd sit in her little room drinking tea and chatting with her while my clothes dried.

I'll never forget Flo and her kindness. She even repaired my jeans when they were torn. She became more than a friend. She was a point of stability, a warm little island where I could seek refuge after drifting around vagrant London.

I made another friend, Molly. It was Molly who showed me how to solve my cash problem. She was a prostitute, a successful one with her own flat above a shop in Soho, and a high-class clientele who saw her by appointment so that she did not have to solicit around the streets.

We met in a snack bar. I had bought a hot dog, but I had an accident with the tomato sauce and it slurped all over the plate. I heard a chuckle behind me.

'I've ruined my hot dog,' I said.

'Well, buy yourself another one,' said this girl who spoke with a lovely soft Irish accent.

'I can't. I've run out of money.'

'Let me buy you one,' she said. 'Or have something else if you like. I'm having fish and chips.'

We sat down and ate our fish and chips together. She was such a warm friendly girl I took to her immediately. I began to tell her some of my problems about difficulties in finding a job.

She laughed, a deep throaty laugh, and said: 'There are ways that a pretty girl can make money in London.'

I did not feel that she was corrupting me—simply offering advice. I told her I didn't think I would be able to do it. But she said: 'I'll teach you.'

So from then on I had an expert tutor in the skills of prostitution.

She took me away from Piccadilly to the quieter pavements north of Oxford Street, and there she gave me my first lessons. She showed me how to swing my

hips in that provocative way that instantly labels a
woman for sale.

It was all right for Molly. She was slim and slinky.
But I was a dumpy little thing. I just couldn't get the
walk right.

'No,' she said. 'Don't put your hand on your hip like
that. You look like a tart.'

'But I am a tart.'

'I know,' she said. 'But I want you to be a classy
one.'

Our first practical lesson was a failure, so she took
me back to her flat to set me right on the theory. I
needed to wear make-up, she said, and I must get some
clothes, interesting clothes, so that men would notice
me.

Molly gave me a shopping list. I'd need a tight skirt,
fairly short, and a white blouse.

It was all very well having a shopping list but I had no
money. That situation was soon resolved. I knew my
friends on the Dilly went on regular shoplifting exped-
itions. They stole gear from the stores which they sold.
A pair of them agreed to take me with them and show
me how it was done.

We went to C & A's. They walked around the coun-
ters arm-in-arm like a pair of young lovers shopping for
their honeymoon. I trailed at a discreet distance behind
watching their every move. The girl took clothes off the
rails and took them into the changing room to try on. I
noticed she was getting a whole lot of items from dis-
play rails in different areas of the shop.

They were cool. The lad would say: 'No, I don't like
that. Try a different colour. Have you got any white
ones?' The girl kept bobbing out of the cubicle saying
she didn't like this, and that didn't suit her.

Eventually she came out in her jeans and sweater.
She bought nothing and left behind an extremely exasp-

erated assistant with heaps of clothes to return to the rails. I followed them out. They had been walking very slowly and casually but in the street they put a sudden spurt on. I had to run to keep up with them.

At the end of the street they stopped and waited for me. The girl lifted up her baggy sweater. Underneath she was wearing two blouses. The boyfriend had a rolled up skirt in his pocket. Underneath her own scruffy jeans the girl was wearing a brand new pair.

So that was how it was done! I thanked the pair of them for a useful lesson which I put into practice the next day. It went like a dream. I even added my own little touch for good measure.

I ordered lots and lots of skirts and blouses, just as I had been instructed, so the shopgirl couldn't keep a tally on them. One black skirt I rolled up tightly and put in my plastic shopping bag. I pushed the bag under the gap into the next cubicle. And I left the cubicle telling the assistant I hadn't fancied anything, but I was wearing a nice white blouse under my sweater.

Then I said to the assistant: 'Where's my shopping bag?' She actually helped me look for it. She found it and handed it to me as I mumbled something about the wrong cubicle. I walked out, slowly and casually just like the other girl, with my shopping bag containing the skirt, a bra and a couple of pairs of panties, all stolen.

At the time I was quite proud of myself. But I don't think shoplifters would get away using those methods today. Assistants in stores are much more wary, and they have electronic tagging and other security devices to protect their goods.

Today I see shoplifting for what it is—a serious crime. But in those days, even though as yet I was not in Satan's clutches, performing a criminal act didn't bother me. I had no conscience about it.

That evening I went to Molly's flat, had a bath, did

my hair and dressed up in my new gear.

Molly looked at me critically. 'Hmm. That'll do. Come on, now. To work.'

We went out into the street and strolled around together until we saw a man hovering at a corner. He was obviously a punter, as we called customers.

Molly whispered to me: 'Off you go now. Don't forget the hips. Wiggle them!'

I walked along the edge of the kerb, and wiggled past the man, just as Molly had told me to. I stood there waiting.

He sidled up to me. 'How much?' he whispered.

I didn't have a clue what he was talking about. Molly had covered everything else in her how-to-be-a-street-walker course. But there were one or two important areas she hadn't mentioned. One was how much I was to ask for—I had no idea. So I took to my heels and ran back to her.

She was doubled up laughing. When she was able to talk, she said: 'What went wrong? He looked a likely one.'

'He asked me how much, and you never told me what I should charge him.'

There were, as I said, a few other points she had slipped up on. Even if I had known what I was supposed to charge, I didn't know where I was to take my customers, or what I was to do for them. Molly had to give me several more lessons on the theory before I dared to venture out again.

Molly was fun, but I didn't enjoy being a prostitute, and I knew I could never graduate to Molly's level. She had style. I was a shop doorway girl with a fiver at the end of it.

No matter how hard I tried, I never became street-wise. So when I was out working, punters were uncertain about approaching me because they were unsure whether I was on the game. And I was never sure which men I should approach in case they were not punters. It was quite bizarre, really.

I only went hustling when I was short of money, and as soon as I'd made some, that was me finished for the night. I didn't go on like the career girls, accumulating wealth so I could get myself a flat and build up a regular clientele.

I didn't much like the men I went with. Most of them were pathetic creatures, and I felt sorry for them. But that didn't stop me stealing their wallets if they had had a few drinks and I thought I could get away with it.

Theft, to me, was preferable to prostitution. My heart wasn't in the game, and even though Molly had selected me as an apprentice with potential, she realised eventually she had picked a dud.

'You're too fussy,' she would say when I moaned about men I went with. Perhaps I was, and I'm glad.

As soon as I had some money, I would go to the Dilly for a chat with my friends. By now I'd found something better to bring on a good mood than the joints we smoked. My friends introduced me to a whole range of different pills. They were cheap, convenient, easy to get hold of, and if a policeman tried to search you you could swallow the whole lot at one go and be on a glorious high.

Other times I would go for a drink. There was a nice friendly little pub that we used just off Curzon Street. It was the sort of place where the staff would let you sit all evening with just one drink if you were out of funds, as I often was. All sorts of people turned up there. Without a fixed address, I needed a focal point, and I suppose that pub was it.

One night I caught the eye of two women who had been looking at me. They were well-dressed, both in their early thirties, and they were nicely made up with expensive hair-dos. At first I thought they were brass, high-class, not like me. But there was something about them that made them stand out from the other customers—some quality I sensed but couldn't define.

I got into conversation with them. They were swish and assured—and generous. They gave me cigarettes and bought me drinks, and, after some chatter, they invited me to a party to be held a few days later in Chelsea.

I didn't dress up. I went along in the usual tatty jeans and sweater. The address was a smart one, and, inside, it was even smarter. There was plenty of food and drink, and a jolly crowd to talk to.

The two women were there. They introduced themselves as Diana and Shirley. I couldn't get over how wealthy and sophisticated they seemed—and that they were taking an interest in me.

After a few drinks, I was high, and I began to quiz them.

'What do you do? Where do you get the money to buy such fine clothes? How can you afford this sumptuous lifestyle?'

They laughed and fended off my cheeky questions. But a little later Diana took me on one side while I was eating a sandwich.

'All of this is available to anyone who really wants it,' she said. 'How badly do you want it?'

'Very badly,' I said, stuffing a sandwich into my mouth. 'I'm fed up with scratching around for money. I can't even afford a proper place to live.'

'There is a way for you to get absolutely anything you want, everything you ever dreamed of.'

She wouldn't tell me any more. I plied her with questions, but all she would say was that she would tell me more another time.

At that first party, I was invited to another party the

following week. It was at a different address—in Fulham. Again there were lashings of food and drink, and Diana and Shirley arrived.

The pair of them looked even more stunning. I looked at my scruffy jeans thinking: 'Why can't I look like that?'

They made a bee-line for me and gave me nice welcoming smiles. For a while we just passed pleasantries. But I was itching to get on to the subject we had touched on at the last party, and they knew it. They were like a couple of clever anglers. They had laid the bait and they were just waiting for me to nibble.

I hesitated. Then, after another drink, I launched into it.

'You said you'd tell me how to get wealth and power. Well, how about it?'

They looked at each other and smiled. Then Diana began to explain.

'A group of us meets every month in a place called Virginia Water. We've been watching you—we think you'd fit in nicely. But you can't just walk in and join. You've got to be initiated. And it's all very secret. You'll have to swear never to tell a soul.'

She never mentioned witchcraft. But somehow, as she spoke, her words conjured up an eerie atmosphere. And her unblinking eyes bored into me like searchlights, hunting out any possible weaknesses.

'I'm very interested,' I said, accepting one more of her cigarettes. 'Tell me how to get there.'

'If you catch the train, we'll pick you up at the station and take you to the place where we hold our meetings.'

I was getting quite excited at the prospect of money and power and the other things they told me I could achieve. I even started spending this great fortune in my mind—within seconds I'd bought the Isle of Wight and an ocean-going yacht.

'When do I come?' I asked excitedly.

Diana said: 'October 31st. Halloween night.'

The penny didn't drop. At Dr Barnardo's we didn't celebrate Halloween. I had no idea it was the most important date in the witch's calendar.

5

'Do You Promise to Serve

the Master?'

The two girls I had met at the parties were waiting for me when the train pulled in. I had heard of Virginia Water, a posh place in Surrey where many important people lived—celebrities, pop stars, wealthy businessmen. I was looking forward to seeing some of their houses, but by early evening it was almost dark and I saw hardly anything as the car whisked us along the leafy country roads.

It was October 31st, 1961, a night that would be for ever engraved in my memory.

As we drove along, I was a little apprehensive. It was like setting out on an adventure with an element of danger and surprise. It gave me a thrill, a sense of excitement and of the unknown.

One of the girls who had met me, Diana, was a doctor. She was dark-haired and very sophisticated. The other was Shirley. Both of them were older than me, in their early thirties, and both as always were immaculately turned out with smart clothes and hair-dos. Beside them I felt out of place in my scruffy old jeans and sweatshirt.

We were not in the car for long before it pulled up at a house. I couldn't see much of the outside but inside it was luxurious. It was Diana's home. The furniture and carpets and decorations must have cost the earth. They were the sort of things I had only ever seen in shop windows in the West End.

They gave me a cup of tea, and then Diana, who seemed to be in charge, came out with an unexpected question—would I like a bath? It was more of an order than a request, but I didn't mind. It was a little while since I had my last free one at Victoria Station.

The bathroom was superb—the suite was a pale green. It was absolute luxury soaking in those scented bubbles. I must have been there an hour before Diana came and told me there was a meal waiting downstairs.

She put out clean clothes for me—just jeans, underwear and a shirt—and I left my dirty things in the bathroom. We went downstairs to a chicken salad. Diana and Shirley were drinking wine, but I was only offered orange juice. It didn't bother me. I was quite happy. Later I discovered that a new member of a coven, at her initiation, must have no trace of alcohol in her system.

As the evening went on, the two women seemed to become more agitated. The phone rang several times. It was always Diana who picked it up. She seemed to be in charge of the arrangements.

I still felt a bit nervous, even though they tried to put me at ease. I remember smoking an awful lot of cigarettes. Both of them were smoking, too, but not as heavily as I was. There was a rack of classy magazines, and I was quite happy flicking through them.

The evening went by, and the time was getting towards midnight when Diana asked me to go back up to the bathroom with her. She brought out a white robe and asked me to put it on, taking off my underwear.

I thought I would be cold, just wearing that with nothing underneath, but I wasn't. It was made of some silky material, swishing as it moved, and fastened with a tie belt, and it came down almost to my ankles. She gave me some white sandals to put on my feet, and we went back downstairs.

There was a car waiting outside, a large luxurious car, with a man driving. One of the women put a coat over my robe so I wouldn't be cold. I got into the back of the car with Shirley who produced a blindfold and told me to put it over my eyes. She must have seen my anxiety, for she quickly added that everybody had to do the same for their first meeting. So I did.

We were driving for six or seven minutes before we pulled up. I couldn't see the place then because I was still wearing the blindfold. But I saw it later. It was a large house with its own drive. The girls led me alongside the house to another building before they took off the blindfold and I was able to see where I was.

I was inside the witches' temple. For the first time I felt a quiver of fear. A tiny voice inside me warned: 'Now Audrey, what have you let yourself in for?' But it was too late to back out. Anyway, I had the feeling I wouldn't have been allowed to.

The building was obviously purpose-built. There was an altar at one end, and the altar cloth, purple in colour, had a golden pentagram emblazoned on it. There was another pentagram, much larger, set out in tiles on the floor.

There was very little light, just two black candles flickering at either side of the altar. A heady, sickly-sweet smell from burning incense filled the room. The place was warm and there was a heavy air of expectancy.

It took a little while for my eyes to become accustomed to the poor light and to make out what was happening. There were a lot of shadowy figures around, between twenty and thirty altogether, all of them in hooded robes.

Eleven of them were standing in a semi-circle facing the altar, with a gap in the middle. The others were standing behind. Later I found out why—the eleven were members of the coven I was to join, thus making up the twelve. The others were guests from other covens who had been invited along—an initiation on Halloween night is an important function.

I was gently but firmly steered towards the gap in the front row. I noticed that all the other women were wearing black robes. I was the only one in white.

We stood there in silence for a minute or two. Then from the side of the hall, a man appeared. He too was all in black, a large hood masking most of his face. He took his place behind the altar, facing the witches. They all knelt down, leaving me, the only one, standing.

What I could see of his face was deathly pale and skeletal, the face of a man in his early forties. The most striking feature was his eyes. They were dark and sunken. Looking at them I felt I was staring into two black holes. It made me shudder.

I remember thinking perhaps I too should be kneeling like all the others. I was conscious of being the odd one out, and it seemed to focus attention on me and make me feel a little afraid. But then all the others got up and started chanting.

It was a strange sound. Some of the words I recognised but others seemed to belong to a curious language that I couldn't recognise. The chanting got louder, like war drums in the jungle. The only phrase that I could pick out was 'We welcome you, O master.' They sang this several times.

The chanting got faster and louder, and it built up a sense of excitement, and anticipation. It was contagious. I got caught up in it—it was impossible to remain unaffected.

Suddenly, as if at a signal, the chanting stopped. Then the warlock reached under his cloak and produced his athame, the special ceremonial dagger used in such ceremonies. He laid it on the altar. Then those black bottomless eyes swivelled round and he spoke. He had a smooth voice with a slight cockney accent.

'Where is the initiate?'

The two witches at either side of me gently pushed me forward.

He looked at me searchingly. I was conscious of my heartbeat speeding up as I stood, the only one in white, in the middle of the semi-circle just in front of the altar.

'Do you want to be initiated?' he asked.

I can't remember saying anything beyond a mumble, which was taken as a yes.

There was a long pause. He liked to take his time and savour his words. Then he said: 'Do you promise on your life to serve the master at all times in obedience?'

All I had to say was yes, so I said yes.

I then had to step forward to the altar. He picked up his dagger and took hold of my left arm. He pricked the wrist and drew a tiny quantity of blood which he collected in a little pot, about the size of a thimble.

Then he laid out a parchment. I didn't read it all, but, having seen such documents since, I know what the words were: 'I am no longer my own. Satan is my master. I live to serve him only.'

He dipped the athame into the blood and motioned me to hold the end of it. With me still holding it, he made a mark on the parchment. I didn't even have to write my name or initials, simply scratch the dagger across the parchment so that it left a smudge of my blood.

When I had done that, he took the knife and laid it back on the altar. Then he addressed me, telling me my coven name was Luci (supposedly the fallen half of Lucifer).

He then reached out and turned me round to face the other witches. They began chanting again. I felt quite relieved. I thought that was it: I was in and the ordeal was over.

The warlock moved away from the altar and returned

with a silver chalice. Then he intoned in that bland cockney accent: 'Who brings the sacrifice?'

I was a little bit perturbed, as this was something I had not expected. I had visions of a cockerel, or perhaps a cat, being brought to the altar. One of the women in the semi-circle stepped forward. She was holding a baby. I hadn't noticed it earlier. It hadn't made a sound during the ceremony. The woman stepped up to the altar, unwrapped the child from its shawl, and laid it naked on the altar.

It was a baby girl, nine days old as I later discovered. She lay on the altar without making a sound, as if she was drugged or something.

Though the room was stiflingly hot, I began to feel cold. I could feel the goosepimples rising at what I was now anticipating. I couldn't really take it in. I couldn't believe what I was seeing. One minute I was all heady and caught up in the excitement and the throb of the chant; then I felt my legs turning to jelly.

The warlock picked up the dagger while muttering a sort of ritualistic speech, something like, 'We offer this sacrifice and hope it pleases you.' Then, with no more emotion than a butcher shows when he's slicing off a steak, he cut the baby's throat.

I thought I was going to pass out. I just stood there and turned absolutely numb. I watched him take the chalice and catch the blood as it gushed from the gaping wound.

The baby's body was taken off the altar and carried away by her mother. The warlock raised the chalice to his lips and drank the still-warm blood. He then moved around from behind the altar and handed the chalice to the witch on the left of the semi-circle. She raised it to her mouth and after taking a sip passed it to the next witch, who then passed it to her neighbour.

Soon it was my turn. The terror of what might happen to me if I fainted kept me on my feet, and the same fear made me raise the chalice and moisten my lips with the baby's blood, revolting though I found it. I could taste the salty flavour on my tongue.

Each of the witches in our coven was handed the chalice, but the guests were not invited to participate. When all twelve of us had taken our turn, the warlock took the chalice back to the first witch. This time he held it while each witch dipped a finger from her right hand into the blood and smudged it on to the left wrist. But he bypassed me, and moved on to the woman on my right. He went right around our coven missing me out of this part of the ceremony.

Even though I had been left out, it soon became obvious that I, the only one in white, was the focus of attention. At this stage, knowing nothing of the ritual, I was ignorant of the Sacrifice of the White Virgin. But I was soon to learn.

The warlock had taken up his place behind the altar again and, as he gazed at me, the other witches began to chant. The two on either side of me then took my elbows and eased me forward. I allowed myself to go, but then I stiffened as the thought occurred to me, 'He's going to kill me. Now it's my turn to be sacrificed.'

The warlock was still staring at me, a strange look entirely devoid of any emotion. I was frightened to look back at him. Then my two escorts tugged at the shoulders of my robe and it slithered to the floor. I stood there naked.

The two witches then moved the black candles to one end, and half lifted me on the altar so that I was lying spreadeagled on my back. The warlock approached me holding the chalice and he began to daub me with the blood, first on my arms and then on the inside of my thighs. He handed the chalice to one of the witches.

I didn't know what was going to happen next, but I had a horrible suspicion. He came towards me, parting his cloak. Underneath he was naked. At that moment I wished he was holding the dagger, and that he would plunge it into my heart. Instead, he raped me.

It's difficult to describe how I felt about it. I suppose most women would have been mortified at the actual sexual aspect of the rape. But to me the sex was not all that important. That part of it was not all that different to what I was doing with men almost every day to get money for drugs. It didn't really bother me.

It was the fact that he showed nothing, no emotions—not even lust—that I found so degrading. That and all those pairs of eyes around the room watching our movements as they continued with their frenetic chanting.

He was sweaty, and there was an unpleasant odour about him. He hadn't been drinking, but his breath and body seemed to exude a strange smell, a little like stale alcohol, as though he'd rubbed himself down with some weird oil or spirit.

I had been with countless men, some of them pretty disgusting. All of them had wanted me, desired my body, or perhaps just needed the body of a woman, any woman. But this man didn't even seem to have need or desire. It was as if something lifeless had entered me, like a walking corpse.

The warlock was a small, wiry man, his hair just beginning to show signs of greying. When he was close to me I was conscious of his yellow teeth. But the eyes were the most frightening feature. I shall never forget them. I couldn't make eye contact with him. They just seemed to go further and further back like voids.

I try now to think back to my own emotions. I know I felt anger that he was raping me in front of all the others, although I realised afterwards that each of them, in their turn, must have had to put up with the same experience. He was our master, and he could call upon us when he wished.

But, looking back, my main feeling soon became one of relief. At least he hadn't killed me. I was also pleased, in retrospect, that I wasn't a virgin. Had I been, the ordeal would have been much worse.

It was most peculiar. I was there. This was really happening. Yet, I suppose because of the fear and the trauma of it all, I was able to detach myself from it, and see it as if I was looking in from the outside.

When he had finished, he got up and I got up and stood by the altar. I was handed a robe, but not the white one I had been wearing. It was a black robe. Another witch put an inverted black cross around my neck. They were all saying: 'Welcome, Luci,' and hugged me and greeted me into their midst.

I was in a daze, but the part of the ritual in which I was at centre stage was now over. The coven had other business to attend to. One of the witches complained that somebody had upset her, and she called upon the warlock to put a curse on whoever it was.

He moved from the altar and stood in the middle of the pentagram on the floor, surrounded by members of the coven. He was mumbling words I didn't understand from some strange language, calling on the powers of darkness.

Then he turned to one of the witches and said, 'Your problem is solved.' He meant he had put a curse upon the offending party but after what I had been through my memory is hazy and I wasn't really aware of who was being cursed, or the reason for it.

That concluded the night's business, and the warlock, the thirteenth member of the coven, simply walked out of the room through a door behind the altar. The rest went into a different room where they removed their robes and put on their clothes. I followed meekly behind. I was handed my own clothes—the dirty jeans and sweatshirt I was wearing when I left London.

There wasn't much chatter. That was something I discovered later—the witches do not socialise or have anything to do with each other outside meetings of the coven. But I did overhear one fragment of conversation. One of the witches asked, 'What's happened to the baby?' and somebody replied: 'It's been burned.'

It didn't make much impact on me at the time. I had seen so much, and so much had happened to me, that the fate of the child's body seemed insignificant.

The mother's name was Mary. She didn't seem at all bothered by what had happened to her baby daughter as she got dressed. I didn't know at that time that babies born to the coven, and fathered by the warlock, are bred to be sacrificed.

That is the whole purpose of having them, and they are sacrificed before they are registered so they are not missed by society.

If I expected the same welcome, the same hospitality, the same friendly fuss, as Diana and Shirley had shown earlier when they met me, I couldn't have been more mistaken. Now I was one of them, and I soon found out I had to find my own way.

A luxurious car had brought me, but there wasn't even a bike to take me away. When I was dressed, in the scruffy old clothes of a London layabout, I was shown the door without being told when we were to meet again, or even given a friendly goodnight.

It was between one and two o'clock in the morning. I walked down from the house on to a road. There wasn't a soul about to ask the way, or any traffic to hitch a lift. But one thing was certain: no way was I going back to ask for directions.

I struck off along the road not really knowing where it would lead me. But my head was in a whirl and I didn't much care. My mind kept flashing back to that baby having its throat cut. Had it been real, or was it all a bad dream? I knew the answer.

I quickened my stride. I wanted to get as much distance between me and that house of horrors as I could. But eventually, after I had been walking an hour or more, tiredness overcame me. I crawled under the hedge of one of those posh suburban houses and went to sleep.

The rumbling traffic woke me early. I stretched, brushed myself down and stepped out to hitch a lift. The driver was going to London. He dropped me off near the Embankment where I was living at that time.

Several times on the journey, and when I was walking along by the river, I pinched myself and wondered had it really happened? Had a baby really been murdered? Had I really been raped? Or was it all some dreadful nightmare, perhaps a trip after popping some of the hallucinatory pills I sometimes took?

I'd like to think it hadn't happened. But it had. The memory was so fresh it hurt. The smell of the warlock was still in my nostrils. Those hymns to Satan the witches had sung so enthusiastically were still ringing in my ears.

As the day went on, I was gripped by more ominous thoughts. These people were powerful. They could harm those who threatened them. They could put a curse on anyone who failed to carry out their will. It occurred to me I might be in danger.

What could I do? Going to the police would be a waste of time. They had been clever enough to ensure I knew no names—and I couldn't identify the house because I had been blindfolded.

The coppers knew me—a young junkie who had often been warned for soliciting. Would they believe me if I told them I had seen a baby having its throat slit? I doubt it. How much notice would they take if I reported I'd been raped by a man in a long black cloak? Not very much.

The more I thought about it, the more I came to

realise I was trapped. In my head I had this frightening, dangerous knowledge, and the only people I could share it with were my fellow witches. Yes, my fellow witches: I was one of them now, and there was no escaping that fact.

One of them had said as I was leaving the house they would be in touch with me to tell me about the next meeting of the coven. All I could do was wait. But there was one way I knew to make the waiting easier and to relieve the pain that seemed to be welling up in my head to the point where I thought it would explode. I turned up from the Embankment into Trafalgar Square and headed for the West End. I needed some pills, and I knew where I could get them. At least they would alleviate my headache, although they would never erase the memory of what I had seen that terrible night. That will stay with me for ever.

6

Life Membership

London, they say, is a lonely place, but I never found it so. If you're living the sort of life that I was in those days, you soon make friends. Perhaps I should call them partners in adversity, or comrades in crime. But they were still my friends.

We'd steal together, and do all sorts of tricks, conning people, bilking on the buses and tubes. But among ourselves was a sort of honour. We'd never steal from each other. In fact, we used to share food, drink, fags, money and drugs—especially drugs.

It was part of the unwritten code that if you had more drugs than essential for your immediate needs, you shared with your friends. Then, when you were short, you could rely on them to reciprocate.

Drugs were becoming the most important thing in my life—more important than food. Funny, I never bothered much about food. There was no such thing as a regular meal. When we got hungry, we'd steal. We'd spend our few coppers on a cup of tea, and while the snack bar proprietor was pouring it, we'd nick a sandwich or a bread roll.

Hot dog stalls were popular. If there were two of you, you'd order a hot dog and drop it when the bloke behind the counter handed it to you. You'd rant a bit, and, if he wasn't wised up, he'd give you another. You'd pick the hot dog up off the ground and there you were—two hot dogs for the price of one.

When you're sleeping together at railway stations, or sharing a cardboard box on the Embankment with people of your own age and lifestyle, you make friends, good friends. The gang I was with were great. But I never told any of them about my night at Virginia Water, even though we shared everything else. I suppose I was scared in case the other witches got to hear I had been shooting my mouth off. But I think there might have been more to it than simply fear.

I had wanted to become a witch. Nobody had forced me to go to that coven. And I was quite pleased to be one. I wanted the powers I thought witches had, possibly because all my life I'd never had any power.

From my earliest days in the children's home, I'd been ordered about and sat upon and never given any responsibility. I wanted the power to manipulate people, and the power that I would gain through witchcraft seemed the only sort available.

So I kept my secret from the rest of the gang, even though I depended on them, and sometimes they on me, for supplies of drugs. My membership of the coven, and the power it gave me, was something I was not prepared to share.

After that first meeting in Virginia Water, my head was whirling. I went to the West End and then to a little café in Victoria where the proprietor dealt in amphetamines, or black bombers as we called them. Just one gave you a high—I took a handful and I was on a high for days.

Eventually, the dreadful things that had happened that night began to fade a little from my mind, and I went back to the old routine. When I was short of money, I'd find a punter prepared to give me a fiver for a quick session, or steal something from one of the big stores and sell it.

There were plenty of Fagins around then—and I suppose there are now—who would gladly take anything we'd stolen, give us a pittance for it, and resell it for a handsome profit. But we were grateful for small sums. They all went towards the next high, anyway.

In those days the pushers were charging half-a-crown for a black bomber. Technically, that's 12½ pence, but in real terms more like £2.50 now. One or two a day would keep me soaring. Purple hearts were cheaper, about a shilling (5 pence) each, but they were not so effective. A slimming drug was also popular—at that time you could easily get it on prescription from almost any doctor.

Later, with the help of my new friends in the coven, I graduated to heroin. But before then, there was a varied and potent menu available to anyone with a few coins to jingle in their pockets, and it helped me forget the frightful things I had witnessed.

The trouble with drugs, as I know now but didn't then, was how one leads to another. I took the black bombers so that I could suppress the hurtful memories of the coven, but they kept me awake. So I had to get my hands on barbiturates to get to sleep.

Most of my life was spent hanging around the West End and Victoria, with my best pals, Shera and Dot, and sometimes Molly. We spent a lot of time in a little pub near Curzon Street. Sometimes, when we were broke, we'd have one glass of beer and four straws.

I had no address, no belongings, no family, and a hunger for drugs. In a jungle like London, you soon learn the tricks of survival—thieving, scrounging, conning, and soliciting. But the secrets of the coven I kept to myself. I didn't even tell Molly and, out of all my friends, she was the one I most trusted.

When she wasn't using her flat for business she often let me sleep there. But in spite of this bond between us, she probably wouldn't have believed me if I had told her about that night in Virginia Water.

But it wasn't just that people might not believe me that stopped me telling. I wanted to protect my fellow witches. If they could show me the path to power and money, the last thing I wanted to do was to destroy them. Even though their evil deeds had shocked and disgusted me, I had gone there as a willing party.

One night, three or four weeks afterwards, I got a sudden blinding headache. It just wouldn't go away, whatever I took for it. I tried lying on the bed in Molly's flat. But the fierce pain persisted, like a pneumatic drill biting into my brain.

Then a voice came to me telling me to be at Highgate Cemetery just before midnight. I tried not to listen. I did my best to get to sleep. But the headache persisted, and so did the voice in my mind. It was so insistent that I had to get up, get dressed, and get on a tube train to Highgate.

I had never been to Highgate or the cemetery before. I didn't even know of it, even though it is famous as Karl Marx's burial place. I didn't know the way when I got off the train—but I didn't need to ask. That voice gave me directions and, just before midnight, I found myself at the cemetery gates, called there by the witches.

I wasn't the only one. There were a number of figures huddled around the gates. Normally they were kept locked, but someone had opened them, and we trooped through making our way to a corner of the vast graveyard.

I recognised some of the witches from Virginia Water. The warlock was there—I'd hardly be likely to forget him—and so was Mary, the mother of the sacrificed baby. Diana and Shirley, the pair who had met me at the station were there. Altogether, I'd say there were between thirty and forty of us.

Somebody had brought our robes, and I was handed one. But we didn't undress—I was glad about that because it was quite a cold night. We gathered around one of the large stone tombs with heavy slabs on top. Somebody spread a cloth with the pentagram on it, and black candles were lit.

This meeting was quite different from the one at Virginia Water. There was no alcohol at that one. But this night there was a lot of boozing. Most of the witches had brought a bottle along, and whisky and gin were being passed around to anyone who wanted them.

There was a lot of chatter and merriment. It didn't seem like a coven. But then we were called to order and one of the warlocks—altogether there were four or five men there—stood on the grave in the circle at the centre of the pentagram, and began to call on the powers of darkness.

Then he got down and two other men went forward. The two of them were able to slide the huge stone slab covering the tomb to one side. It must have required tremendous strength, but they moved it quite easily. The warlock had been calling upon Satan to give them this strength.

One of the warlocks vanished inside the tomb. He was out of sight for about fifteen minutes. Then he reappeared holding a skull. This, it seems, was the purpose of the meeting: one of the covens required a skull for their rituals. I never found out why they wanted it, but skulls are often used in witchcraft. Some covens make do with animal skulls, but a human skull is thought to be more powerful.

Apart from the opening of the grave and the taking of the skull, there was almost a party atmosphere at that meeting. People were drinking quite heavily, including me, and many of the witches were hugging and kissing. There is a lot of lesbianism in witchcraft—I think many women join covens because the female predominance means they will find others of the same sexual inclination.

I had a lot to drink and I can't remember how the meeting ended. But I must have found my way back to Molly's flat, because that was where I woke up the next day. I remember thinking perhaps this witchcraft was not so bad after all. I'd seen and done terrible things that first time, but the night in the cemetery had been almost a social occasion with everyone chatting happily over a drink.

It was early in the New Year when I next heard from the coven. The New Year doesn't have any special significance for witches. They have their own New Year—Beltane, which is May Day.

The witches knew I hadn't got a regular address, but some of them knew the pub I used off Curzon Street. That was where they had first of all spotted me before inviting me to the parties where, though I didn't know it at the time, I was screened as a potential recruit.

I went into the pub one night and the barman called me over.

'Are you Luci?' he asked.

I said that was a name some people called me.

'There's a message for you.'

He handed me a slip of paper. The message simply said 'Virginia Water' and gave a date. It didn't need to say any more. The time was always the same—shortly before midnight. I assumed that if I caught the last train out there, someone would meet me and take me to the venue.

The assumption was correct. A taxi driver who had been given my description met me and drove me to a house which turned out to be unoccupied. We had several meetings subsequently in empty houses. It was this that led me to believe our warlock might be an estate agent, for I cannot think how else he could come by all the keys.

The driver dropped me and drove away. The fare had obviously been looked after. The door was open and I walked in. The rest of the coven were already there. Although the pentagram was on the floor, there was no altar. I soon learned there was to be no ritual that night—just lessons in Satan worship.

Somebody arrived with the robes and distributed them. This was a regular job, I discovered, for one of the witches. Various tasks were allotted around the members of the coven, and the mistress of the robes (I don't remember her exact title) had to make sure all the black cloaks were at the chosen venue.

The warlock began his teach-in by telling us that if we pleased the master, he would give us what we wanted. And then, for the first time, I saw a demonstration of Satan's amazing power. One of the girls went into the circle in the centre of the pentagram. The warlock was standing behind her at one of the points. She began to chant, a weird mumbling, unlike anything I had heard before.

She began by standing, then she sat, and the next minute she was up in the air. I just looked at her. I couldn't believe it. I had never even heard of levitation. But here she was, several feet above the ground. She stayed there for several minutes. Then she slowly came back down to the floor.

People I've told about this find it very hard to believe. How can anyone defy the force of gravity? they ask. But there are many ancient faiths which claim to give followers the power of levitation. It is something practitioners of transcendental meditation claim they can achieve. If they have these powers, who can say that Satan doesn't also have them?

I wanted to ask this witch how she had done it. But I

didn't dare. I was still a little timid in the company. Then another woman went into the circle and did the same thing.

I was then invited to sit in the circle. I did. But nothing happened. Then the warlock said: 'You are not calling on the powers.'

So I stood up, and I said: 'Now if you are really the master, show me.'

I stood there. And then, very, very, slowly, I rose a few inches off the ground. I thought to myself, 'Crumbs, what are you doing?' Then I came back down with a bump. I had done it. I had levitated—although I didn't know how.

Afterwards, I went up to the first witch who had levitated and asked her how she'd done it. She was friendly and helpful. She said: 'You have to train your mind. You have to empty it completely and concentrate on Satan and his power will lift you up.'

When I left, I had to make my own way to the station which was only a short distance away. The last train had gone, so I kipped down to wait for the first morning train. I was excited. Witchcraft was starting to do something for me. I was beginning to get the powers I craved. At last I would be a somebody—a force to be reckoned with.

Those monthly teach-ins went on, each time at a different location. They taught me a little more each time about how to call up Satan's powers, and I have to say I found it fascinating. We were taught about the old pagan laws, and shown new rituals. And they began to take me into their trust.

Eventually I was given a telephone number where I could ring one of the senior witches, Diana, and ask her for details of where the next meeting would be held. But as I had found out the night some mysterious force summoned me to Highgate Cemetery, the coven had their own way of getting in touch without a telephone.

As well as teaching us how to call upon Satan's powers, we were given lessons on the history of witchcraft. I was totally ignorant. I didn't even know the definition of a witch. In British law, a witch is 'a person who hath conference with the devil to consult with him or do some act'.

We were taught that in medieval England there were hundreds of witches. But they were persecuted, tortured and put to death in the sixteenth and seventeenth centuries and had to go underground. Under new laws passed in the early 1950s, it is quite legal to be a witch, and to practise witchcraft. But some of the things we did in that coven in Virginia Water were far from legal.

We were told by our tutor, the warlock, of the four main witchcraft festivals in the year—on February 2 (Candlemas), May eve (Roodmas) August 1st (Lammas) and November eve (All Hallow E'en).

Our coven met much more frequently than on these festivals—almost every month. But special things happened at the major festivals. Already I had witnessed some of them. Before long I was to see many more.

It was at one of those early lessons that we were taught how to communicate with the dead. We were in a coven, all thirteen of us including the warlock. It was just our own cosy group.

The warlock began to go through a long and complicated invocation to bring down the dark powers. I learned it was an ambition of all covens, not just ours, to persuade Satan to reveal himself. It never happened in my experience. But this particular night we had a 'visitor from the dead'.

One of the witches began to cry out. A figure appeared by the side of the warlock, and she recognised it as her departed father. He just stood there with the warlock behind the altar. To me the face was indefinable, but the witch recognised him, and called 'Father!'

He spoke to her. I can't remember what he said but he and his daughter had a conversation. It seemed to be meaningful to her but it didn't make much sense to the rest of us.

I didn't even know who my father was. But I thought this would give me an opportunity to meet him. Twice the warlock tried at my request to bring him back, but it never worked. I was told it was my fault for not believing strongly enough in Satan's powers.

But the levitation was improving. I could get up several feet. I also learned to make articles move without touching them. It was partly a question of mind control. I had to focus my entire thinking on to the object, and call up Satan to help. By practising when I was alone, I got pretty good at it. I could move chairs about and rearrange the furniture without touching it, or make a picture fall off the wall.

I remember calling on a friend of Molly's for tea one day. While the old lady was brewing up in the kitchen, I thought I'd practise a little bit of witchcraft by moving her furniture around.

Her face was a picture when she carried in the tray with the cups and teapot and found the table had moved. I didn't let on, of course. The poor old dear thought she was going out of her mind.

As with levitation, this is an aspect of witchcraft that people just cannot grasp. I don't think I would be able to if I hadn't seen it with my own eyes and possessed the power, albeit at a low voltage, to do it myself.

The supernatural aspects of life are hard to understand. Communication with the dead, ghosts, poltergeists, telepathy—many people are sceptical about all of these powers unless they have experienced them.

Why this should be, I do not know. Christians do not find it difficult to believe Jesus was capable of performing miracles, or in God's powers to do good. Is it not equally conceivable that Satan, once a powerful angel until he fell from grace, should have kept the powers God had given him, and now use them for evil?

The way the coven used to communicate with me is an example. Occasionally I would telephone my contact in the coven, or receive a written message via the barman in the pub. But most of the time we didn't use phones, or write messages. It would be by telepathy—a feeling in my head that something was being arranged. And it was never wrong. When Satan sends a message, he doesn't get the wrong number.

You can imagine the disbelief on the faces of the two policemen when, years later, I made a full confession. Telepathy? Levitation? Bringing back the dead? These occult practices are well outside the understanding of most policemen. But anyone who is a Christian, and appreciates God's powers, will have no difficulty in accepting there are dark powers as well, controlled by Satan.

After they had attended a few covens and gained the trust of the warlock and their sisters, most of the witches were given a task. Soon I was given my first assignment. It was nothing too difficult. A party was being organised, and I was told to bring along a number of guests.

Diana, who gave me my instructions, was quite specific about numbers, and ages, and sexes. I had to find about twenty people, mostly girls but some boys, and their ages must be between thirteen and eighteen.

For somebody who knew London well, as I did, the job presented no difficulties. There were dozens of kids hanging around the cafés, amusement arcades and railway stations, many of them runaways, and they would eagerly go anywhere for a few drinks and some free food—with the promise of some drugs, music and a good time—including the chance of sex.

When I was given the task, I assumed it was to recruit these youngsters, or some of the selected ones, into the coven. It didn't occur to me that some of them, just thirteen, or fourteen, were too young. I suppose I thought the very young ones were being marked down as future witches.

Youngsters who had run away from home could always be found at the railway stations. Had it been a man meeting them, they would have been suspicious. There were always so many pimps about eager to recruit girls, and boys, as prostitutes. But with me, a woman, not much older than themselves, they were more trusting.

I'd been given the time, date and venue and I simply passed it on to likely contenders. If some of them didn't show up, it wouldn't matter. On the night, between twenty-five and thirty did at a nice big flat in Finsbury Park.

There were a few members of the coven acting as stewards and handing out the drinks. But it soon became clear to me that this was no ordinary party, even though the kids seemed to be enjoying themselves.

The drinks, I suspect, were spiked with some drug, probably LSD. That soon took effect. The youngsters began pawing each other. And the witches who were there, obviously lesbians, homed in on the young girls.

Then I detected something more sinister. Candles had been lit, and they were giving off a distinctive odour—heroin.

Afterwards I learned that it was quite a popular trick at drug parties to inject heroin down a candle close to the wick. As it burned down it heated the heroin releasing stupefying fumes into the air. When the youngsters got this in their lungs, they went crazy.

It was almost as if somebody had given an order to peel off their clothes. Soon they were all naked, dancing and caressing in the smokey flickering light. Before long a full-scale orgy was taking place. There were about four men and three or four women there, and they were encouraging the children in sexual excesses. It was all pretty sickening.

But there was worse. I suddenly became aware of flashes of light in different parts of the room. One of the men was taking pictures with a flash camera, and then I noticed one of the women had a camera and was taking pictures as well.

I was puzzled. I'd never come across any photographs at the coven meetings, and I'd been attending them for six months by this time. The two people with cameras seemed to be concentrating on the younger children in various sexual poses. Then the horrible truth dawned on me. There could be only one purpose for these despicable pictures—pornography.

And I was the person whom these young people had trusted to bring them to a party. To introduce them to witchcraft was bad enough. But to use them for pornography was something else.

I felt sick, so sick I had to leave. I almost passed out as I left the smokey room. My head was reeling. I leaned against the wall in the hallway for support, then vomited all over the carpet. I was disgusted with myself.

The pornography racket, I later discovered, was the way the coven made its money. There are wealthy people in high places who will pay a lot of money for sexually explicit pictures of youngsters, and some of the witches needed a sizable income to maintain their lifestyle. This was how they got it.

It may seem ironic that I, a prostitute, should have high principles about commercial sex. Sex among adults was one thing. But corrupting youngsters with drugs and using them for pornography was, to my mind, quite different. I found it appalling, and I resolved I would never again have anything to do with it.

Alas, other people had different ideas. When I made my views known at the next gathering of the coven and told them I was not going to be involved in any more of these wicked parties where children were exploited, the warlock fixed me with a long and angry glare.

'You don't own yourself any more,' he said. 'You belong to us. You belong to Satan. You will carry out his wishes.'

As he spoke, he drew the athame from beneath his cloak, and he continued to finger its sharp point as he glared at me. I knew then that if I continued to refuse, he would kill me with as little compunction as he had slit that baby's throat.

7

'People Always Come Back To Us'

Worshipping Satan had, by now, become the most important activity in my life. I lived for those meetings of the coven. As they approached, I felt a mounting excitement. I felt myself being drawn to them like a tin-tack to a magnet—the force was irresistible.

There were lots of things that the coven did which sickened me. I wanted no part of them. But the power of my fellow witches in action was so compelling, and Satan seemed so strong, I had to be there to see it and participate.

As well as the 'ordinary' monthly meetings of the coven there were special meetings at which quite large numbers of guests appeared. And they brought along young children.

This was the part that sickened me most of all. In the light of the flickering candles, I witnessed horrible sights as those evil people, spurred on by the warlock and witches, abused those children.

There were dreadful lesbian scenes where some of the women used contraptions to sexually interfere with little girls. Others involved young boys in oral sex. The youngsters must have been given some drug to keep them quiet. There were no protests from them, no shouts of pain, no tears.

Some of these hideous outrages took place on the floor

in the pentagram. Others took place on the altar. It was an orgy of perversion. These monstrous people were gratifying themselves with Satan's blessing while the witches provided background music with their strange chanting hymn to the devil.

I remember standing as far back as I could in that satanic temple, set up in an ordinary looking bungalow in Virginia Water. But I knew I couldn't leave.

To have walked away and turned my back on them at that stage would have been to invite the warlock to carry out his threat. If he could kill an innocent baby, I'm sure he would have killed me, a danger who might jeopardise the security of the coven and its operations.

Though I had no proof, I became convinced that the coven was operating a dual role—for the devil worshippers to practise their skills and for the equally sinister purposes of running a child sex racket.

The orgies in the satanic temple used to take place quite frequently every couple of months. The special guests always looked wealthy and well turned out. Sometimes there would be as many as twenty of them, men and women, ages ranging from thirty to sixty. They didn't wear robes like the witches. They were not initiates—they were there purely for the sex.

I never saw money change hands, but I'm positive they paid the warlock, and some of the witches, large sums to supply the children to use for their evil gratification. My reason for believing this was the lifestyle of the coven hierarchy. They must have been getting their money from somewhere, and I always suspected it was from the VIP guests they let loose on the children of the coven.

Later, when the warlock was supplying me with heroin, my suspicions were even stronger. The cost of the drugs he was giving me must have run into many thousands of pounds. He was supplying drugs to other people as well. Heroin does not come cheap, and I'm sure the drug supply was funded out of the profits of child sex.

The fate of the little children didn't matter to the witches. Any babies they bore became the property of the coven, to do with as the warlock thought fit. They were being passed around like playthings for the sport of these perverts.

I swore then that if I ever became pregnant, my baby would never share that awful fate. I would kill it myself before letting that happen, whatever Satan commanded. I have often felt disgusted with myself, but never so strongly as that first night when I was an unwilling witness to those awful scenes of child abuse. But I was afraid that if I walked out I would be killed.

The strange thing about these meetings in Virginia Water was that I was rarely summoned, although occasionally notes were left at the pub where I used to drink off Curzon Street. I had been given the telephone number of Diana's house, and I could ring to check. But most of the time it wasn't necessary. Some inner compulsion told me when, and where, to go.

It was a sort of mounting pressure in my head. I put it down to the strange power of Satan. He wanted me at his meetings—and if you believe in the dark forces, it's not difficult to accept that Satan could direct me to the coven by remote control.

Even after I broke away from the witches, I could still feel this strange pulling in my mind, sometimes so powerful it brought on a raging headache. When events that I consider to be satanic such as occult festivals were advertised, it would stir something up inside my mind and get me absolutely racing with a strange sense of excitement and expectancy.

I only went to three of these 'open meetings' where people from outside the coven came along to abuse children. Two of them took place at the bungalow and the third at another venue, also in Virginia Water. The wealth of these visitors impressed me. There were always lots of new shiny cars parked outside.

Our regular meetings were usually dedicated to study of the history of witchcraft. We would start with a short prayer session, praying to Satan, of course, and sometimes there would be a blood sacrifice. But it was always a cockerel.

In my years as a witch, I never witnessed a second human sacrifice. I did hear of human sacrifices in other covens, but I only ever saw the one at my own initiation. It was enough. The awful memory of it has stayed with me as if it happened yesterday.

There have been mounting suspicions over the years that child sacrifices take place regularly. I believe that they do. I have no evidence to support this belief, but witchcraft and devil worship are on the increase in Britain, and human sacrifice is a recognised tradition in the cult.

At our meetings, there was usually some sexual activity after the study period. I was young and quite nice looking and I had quite a lot of trouble fending off the advances of my lesbian sisters in the coven. One of them was very persistent. She used to keep sliding her hands over me, sometimes trying to get under my robe. I threatened to biff her one night, and I complained to the warlock about her. It worked.

There was also jealousy over who the warlock would choose as his sexual partner. Because I was young, it was usually me, and the other witches used to get steamed up because they wanted him. I didn't find the warlock attractive, but I found him protective. There were even times when I felt pangs of jealousy if he picked someone else as his sexual partner. It wasn't so bad if it was one of the witches in our coven. That didn't bother me, because they had the right, and he had the right. But when we held joint meetings with other covens and he chose someone who was perhaps younger and prettier than me, I felt jealous.

Jealousy is perhaps too strong a word—threatened would be a more accurate description. If he chose somebody else, I used to worry about what might happen to me, and whether I'd be kept in the coven. I needed the coven. It had become a vital part of my life. I had no home or possessions and it was the one thing I felt I could cling to. It gave me a sense of belonging.

Sex with the warlock was not a pleasurable experience. There was always that strange smell about him, as though he rubbed his body with some peculiar acrid chemicals. But I suppose I felt a little bit honoured at being chosen by this powerful man who was our leader. It used to give me a bit of a kick, thinking: 'He's got all these women to choose from—and he chooses me.' But my sex sessions with him were something to be endured rather than enjoyed.

I was, by now, quite an accomplished young witch. I could levitate. I could bring down the powers of darkness to move furniture around. I had attended a dozen or so meetings of the coven, learning more each time and enjoying them, except those awful occasions when they brought young children and abused them. Soon I was looking forward to my first anniversary of joining.

The approach of that Halloween found me getting quite excited. I remembered all too well what had happened to me, and I was curious to see how the coven would celebrate the major night of their calendar, my first as a fully-fledged witch.

The meeting was in the same house where I had been initiated. There was no summons—just the telepathic message buzzing in my head telling me I must be there.

I caught the train down to Virginia Water. There was a taxi waiting there which took me to the house. I'm sure the local taxi drivers must have known something funny was going on—all these strange ladies being picked up and taken to the same large house.

There were two groups there that night, making twenty-four of us, plus the warlock. It started with the same low chanting. What those words were I never knew, even though I found myself singing along and chanting with the other witches. It was as if a foreign language was coming out of my mouth, without my ever having gone to the trouble to learn it. Yet afterwards I wasn't able to repeat a single word of it. I now recognise that that was Satan at work, bestowing on us the power of speaking in strange tongues.

It hadn't occurred to me before that this special night might be the occasion to sacrifice a baby, as had happened at the last Halloween. But when the warlock took up a cockerel and slit its throat, I was very relieved.

I was in my black robe standing just in front of the altar, and I wasn't aware of what was going on behind. Then a girl in a white robe was suddenly pushed into the semi-circle, as I had been a year ago. I knew then exactly what was going to happen.

I found myself studying her face. She was only thirteen, I discovered. She had been picked up on the street by a couple of the witches. She was a pretty little thing with shoulder-length brown hair, and by her glazed eyes it was obvious she had been drugged.

She moved like a zombie when she was thrust forward to have her wrists daubed with blood. I was glad she had been drugged. At least she wouldn't feel any pain when the warlock raped her. And hopefully her memories of the experience would be blurred.

The white robe was slipped from her shoulders and she stood there naked, a tiny pathetic figure, confused and lonely. Two of the witches lifted her onto the altar. She lay there while the warlock raped her. There were no tears, no screams, no protests. It was like watching an old black-and-white horror movie, except that it was for real.

Afterwards, the young girl was lifted from the altar and dressed again in her white robe. She soon disappeared. A couple of the witches took her to put on her own clothes. She was taken away and dumped on the street, somewhere in the suburbs of London, near where she had been picked up.

I never heard anything else about her. If she had parents and complained to them, they obviously didn't go to the police, otherwise we would have read something about it. They probably thought she had been sniffing glue, or taking tablets, and had hallucinated the whole thing. Who would believe such a bizarre story? Who would have believed me if I had trotted out my tale? Even though I was a dedicated witch, wanting to do all I could to please Satan, there were still aspects that distressed and disgusted me. I remember feeling anger about what had happened to this little girl.

True, there were some similarities with what had happened to me when I was the central figure in the Sacrifice of the White Virgin. But I was older, and I had chosen to become a witch. This poor girl had been snatched from the streets, pumped full of drugs, and forced to submit to rape.

She had had no choice. She was an innocent, and that was what angered me. I couldn't come to terms with it, but I tried to put it out of my mind in case Satan should gaze deeply, realise I was nurturing disloyal thoughts, and punish me for them.

It was about this time that I had another growing worry, literally growing inside me. I had suspected I might be pregnant, and now I knew I was. There had been lots of men, some I knew, others I had forgotten. I couldn't be certain, but there was a strong possibility that the father was the warlock.

I had had sex with him about a dozen times, never with my total compliance, and certainly never with love. But the thought that he was probably the father filled me with an awful foreboding.

I had seen a baby being sacrificed. I knew that if the baby I was carrying was allowed to be born, it would finish up the same way. My reaction was that I must get rid of it. The child must not be born. If the warlock discovered I was pregnant, he would claim the child for Satan.

Nowadays, having an abortion is no problem. But this was 1962 before abortions-on-demand were legal, and back street operations had to be arranged. But with the sort of friends I had, streetwise and living on the fringe of the law, finding an abortionist was no problem.

When I was three months pregnant, I went off to a café in Brentwood where, my friends had assured me, I would be looked after. It was all a bit of a farce. The café proprietor claimed he was an abortionist, but he didn't seem to know much about it. We finished up having an affair. By day I worked for him selling beefburgers. At night I slept with him.

One day he came back with some apparatus he had borrowed which he said would get rid of the baby. He fixed up some sort of a douche but the whole thing was a fiasco. We finished up having a blazing row, and he threw me out into the street.

It was in the early hours of the morning, and I was walking around the streets. I was spotted by a police car, and they saw I was in a state so they took me to a hospital. It was a mental hospital, Warley, at Brentwood, and it was the right place for me. After all I had been through, culminating in a failed abortion, my mind as well as my body was in urgent need of treatment.

The police took me there because they feared what I

might do to myself. I told them I had tried to get rid of the baby, and they took out a twenty-eight-day order confining me to the hospital for my own good. But I was there a lot longer than twenty-eight days. I was there for six months – until the baby was born.

Remembering my outburst on the night they picked me up, the police came to question me while I lay in my hospital bed. They had suspected the café proprietor of carrying out abortions, and they thought my evidence would enable them to nail him. But when I started getting agitated the doctor ordered them out, and said I was too ill to be questioned.

I spent Christmas in that hospital. In the past, Christmas had never meant much to me. I had had some pretty miserable ones. But that one at Warley I'll never forget.

With the help of some of the fitter patients the nurses had put up a tree in the reception hall. On Christmas Eve one of the nurses came into my room and asked me to go with her for a walk. She led me to the hall where this huge tree stood, beautifully decorated.

I stood there looking up at the fairy lights, and my mind went back to my time at Dr Barnardo's. We always had a lovely Christmas tree there. Only a few years had passed since I had left Farm Hill. But so much had happened in that time, so many dreadful things, it seemed much longer.

More nurses came in wearing their capes, and other patients joined us for a carol service. They began to sing 'Away in a manger'. I remembered the crib we always set up at Farm Hill, and the nativity plays we used to do.

Once, when I was about six or seven, I had played Mary in our Christmas play. I was carrying a doll, the baby Jesus. Everybody laughed because I was treating the doll like a real baby. I felt the tears trickling down my face as the memories came back, and I felt myself wishing that I could be good, like these nurses, instead of a servant of the devil.

The nurse who had brought me saw the tears. She gently escorted me back to my room. She was a sweet girl. She said: 'Audrey, what's wrong? What's troubling you?'

I would dearly love to have told her. But I didn't dare. I couldn't tell anybody. It was a secret I had to keep to myself. I just said one word to her: 'Memories.'

As well as Christmas, the staff at that hospital remembered it was my birthday. I was given two presents—a sponge bag and a shawl. Nurses and patients sang Happy Birthday when they cut my cake, and I found myself blubbing again. But they were tears of joy.

The six months I was in that hospital seemed a long time, but it flashed by. I was getting regular meals, and building myself up. They were giving me drugs—I don't know what but I assume it was something to settle my mind and stop me feeling too depressed. There seemed plenty to do. I read a lot, and I was able to do some painting which I loved.

I was in a secure ward, and the nurses kept a close eye on me in case I wanted to get away so that I could kill my baby. I would have done anything to prevent that child being born, haunted as I was by the fear that the coven would somehow get their hands on it and offer it to Satan.

I left the mental hospital to go to the local maternity hospital for the birth. But I had kept insisting I didn't want it, and didn't even want to see it. It was taken from me at birth. I say It because I never knew the sex of the child. I still don't. The doctors knew my state of mind, and they agreed it would be better if I was not allowed even to see it.

I didn't even register the child's birth, but I assumed the social services must have done. I hoped the child would be taken to a decent home, and be brought up by adoptive parents who would love and look after it.

It would have a much happier future than with me. I knew the coven would probably know what I was up to—they seemed to know everything about me—but they weren't running after me now and that was all that mattered.

Once the baby was born, my mental illness vanished. With the devil's child nestling in my womb, I had become deranged. But after it had left my body, I returned to normality. In fact, I was so normal the hospital staff helped me to get a job looking after old people at a nursing home in Brentwood. There were no fears that I couldn't handle a responsible position.

There were bright moments, but looking back, this was a dismal period of my life. People will wonder what sort of a woman I was who could forego her natural instincts and give up her child without a thought.

Don't get me wrong. I love children. I loved babies when I was looking after them at Dr Barnardo's. But this child was not mine. It was Satan's. I wanted nothing to do with it. I would have happily killed it myself to save it from an awful death on the coven altar.

The job at the old people's home didn't last for long. I stuck it for about three months. Then I had a row with the matron and just walked out. I went back to my old haunts in the West End for a week or two. Then I decided on the spur of the moment, and for no obvious reason, to go to Southend.

This was the summer of 1963 when I was twenty-three. It was the year of the Profumo scandal and the Great Train Robbery. The trippers were flocking into Southend, and I got caught up in the holiday atmosphere.

The excitement of the coven had, for some reason, worn thin. I didn't feel the need for witchcraft. It was almost as if the birth and loss of the warlock's baby had somehow cleansed me. I was looking for something else away from Satan—normal things like a job and a home.

In Southend I found both. The job was on the buses as a clippie. And I got a flat in a big house in Westcliffe. But before I actually started work, there was a little problem with my rent. I hadn't got any money to pay it, so the landlord, an unpleasant greasy man in his early forties, made a suggestion that was new to me.

He didn't want sex—that I could have understood. But he wanted to come to my room and take some pictures of me. Naked, of course, and not art studies!

I was a bit bothered, so I consulted my neighbours, two lesbians who shared the next flat. They pondered on the problem, and came up with a solution: 'Why not let him if it saves you paying the rent?'

I told them I didn't much fancy the idea, so they said: 'Take some of these.'

Hidden behind a light switch in their room was a stock of pills. They gave me a couple of bombers and I was able to cope. The pictures were taken, I felt fine, and I was able to live rent free until I started work.

I liked working on the buses, and I stuck the job for about six months. For someone who had not had regular money for a long time, the pay was good. Even getting up at four o'clock in the morning for the early shift was tolerable.

I was soon taught the fiddles that go with work on the buses. We never paid for our cups of tea, for example. The money would come straight out of my bag. Then I would have to overcharge on a couple of fares to make it up. All the clippies I knew did this—and many of them, I was to learn, had love affairs with their drivers.

I certainly did with mine. But it came to a sudden stop at the bus company's Christmas party. He brought his wife along. She suspected there was something going on between her husband and me, and we had a stand-up row.

My love life, if you can call it love, was very active during those few months in Southend. I was having an occasional affair with a detective, as well as the driver. He was on the drug squad, and was supposed to be tracking down drug pushers in the area. Little did he know that my lesbian neighbours were pushers—and I was one of their customers.

I was having a ball, but there were still moments of loneliness. I had no real friends, people I could turn to, share my problems with, and chat about things. That is why I was taking drugs, not heavily but regularly. I was taking bombers, amphetamines, and the occasional snort of cocaine, although this was expensive and I could not often afford it.

Again, to help with the loneliness, I took an evening job helping out at a café. But with the drug-taking, boozing, two love affairs, two jobs, lots of late nights, and early starts on the buses, something had to go. I started turning up late for work—and so lost my job on the buses.

What had been a happy but hectic existence suddenly began to pall. Without the bus money, I was soon in financial trouble again. My landlord was breathing down my neck for the rent every week, and I certainly was not going to pay him off again by posing for more dirty pictures.

So one day I decided to pack it all in. I took a fiver out of the till at the café where I was working part-time, money I reckoned they owed me, and bought a single ticket to London.

It was a journey back to my old gang of pals and the lifestyle I thought I had put behind me. By now I needed drugs more and more, and to get the money to pay for them I went back to soliciting, and stealing.

When I was in my little flat in Southend, I had amassed a few possessions—just odd things like books, one or two ornaments, and some clothes. It was the first time I had ever had a place where I could keep my own things. But when I caught that London train, I left them all behind.

Now I was living rough again, finding warmth and a place to sleep wherever I could. But shelter was a second priority. Drugs were the first.

The coven had not featured in my life while I was in Southend. But now I felt I needed to see my fellow witches. Satan was beckoning – and, like a willing lamb, I was answering his call.

I had a telephone number to contact Diana, my recruiting officer for the coven. One night I rang her up to ask her what was happening, and if any meetings were planned in the near future.

'Hello, Luci,' she said sweetly. 'You've been away. But we knew you'd come back. People always come back to us.'

8

Powder, Flame and a Needle

It had happened without my really noticing it, but my
need for drugs was growing every day. There was a time
when I was taking one or two bombers a week, but now I
was greedily swallowing that number every morning, and
wanting more.

They cost money, of course. Sometimes you could
scrounge them off a fellow addict around the Dilly. But
unless you could give them drugs in return, or cash to
buy drugs, those sources soon dried up.

I had saved a little bit of money while working in
Southend, but that was soon gone. I didn't like selling
my body, but it was a means of easy money and that was
how I financed my growing craving.

One of my best clients was a good-looking man, in his
mid-twenties, called Brian. He used to drive a green
sports car. He paid me—and he didn't want sex.

The first time he picked me up, he was driving through
Soho, and stopped near where I was standing. Assuming
he was a client, I jumped into his car and he drove away.
He kept driving all the way to Clapham Common. I was
getting worried. I thought he might be a weirdo – there
were plenty of those preying on young prostitutes.

He pulled up at a quiet part of the common and introduced himself.

'I'm Brian.'

'I'm Audrey.'

It was strange. He wasn't behaving as punters usually do. He didn't ask how much, or anything. Then he asked me: 'Why did you get in the car?'

I replied: 'Well, you're a client, aren't you? I thought you wanted me.'

He shook his head. 'No. I simply thought you wanted a lift or something.'

I was a bit miffed, having been driven all this way. 'So you're not a client?' I said.

'No,' he said. 'And I don't think you're very good at what you're doing. You shouldn't really be at this lark.'

It was a comic misunderstanding, but he gave me a £5 note and drove me back into London. He used to come to the West End regularly, and pick me up. He never wanted anything, except a bit of a chat, and he always gave me a fiver. A good customer—I wished I'd had more like that.

The people I picked up were a mixed bunch. Most wanted sex as quickly as possible and then to be rid of me. Some were lonely and wanted to talk. There were odd balls, too. I remember getting into one car and the driver immediately started talking about whips and bondage. I jumped out at the next set of traffic lights and ran.

Brian's analysis was right. I wasn't a good prostitute. I was too fussy. Instead of taking the money and getting on with the job, I used to reject many potential clients because I didn't fancy going with them.

Molly, my guide and mentor, tried to train me. 'Walk up the path,' she would say, 'and smile at that man on the corner.'

I'd walk up, and then come back.

'What happened?' Molly would say.

'I just didn't fancy him.'

'Oh, you. You'll never make a pro. You're much too fussy.'

She was right. I just didn't see how any girl could go out night after night picking up men by the dozen and sleeping with them. As soon as I had earned enough for a fix, that was me finished—until I needed another fix and had to earn some more.

Drugs were ruling my life and dictating my behaviour. On one occasion I even turned to mugging. It was in Oxford Street. I was desperate for money. There was an old lady walking along in front of me. I knocked her flying and grabbed her bag. There was only two-and-six in her purse – enough for one bomber. But I took it.

That was the first and last time I ever turned to violence to satisfy my craving for drugs. It's a sad memory that has stayed with me. I can still see the look of fear and astonishment on her face as she went down.

Oddly enough, even though I was doing a little bit of burglary, and regularly shoplifting, the first time I got into trouble with the law was for taking something that I felt rightfully belonged to me—that fiver from the till of the café in Southend.

The proprietor had reported it as a theft, even though he owed me more than that in wages. After failing to find me in the streets around Southend, I suppose my name had gone on some wanted list that was circulated to other police forces—even for a fiver.

One evening near Oxford Circus I was approached by a policeman and a policewoman. They asked me if my name was Audrey Wilbraham.

'Yes,' I said. All the criminal things I had been up to flashed through my mind. But it came as a shock when they told me why they wanted me.

'We're arresting you for stealing some money in Southend,' the police officer said.

They took me in a police car to Southend. I was very

tearful on the journey. They didn't know why, but I was suffering from the withdrawal effects of amphetamines. In fact, I had been on my way to a little café to buy some when they stopped me.

The police officers were worried about me, and the state I was in. They had a debate about whether to take me to hospital. But they decided against and took me to the main police headquarters in Southend.

I was charged with taking the five pounds, and put in a cell for the night. They brought a doctor to see me. He suggested that I should get myself admitted to hospital for a course of treatment. I agreed that I would, and he gave me an injection to knock me out for the night.

The following morning I appeared before the magistrates. I admitted taking the money, and I was fined £10. But all thoughts of admitting myself to hospital were forgotten. I scooted back off to London as quickly as I could, dodging paying the fare as I usually did when I hadn't any money.

About this time, there was a curious interlude in my life, a respite from drugs and soliciting, begging and burglary, and the awful filth and squalor that I had become accustomed to.

I was walking down Oxford Street in the early hours one morning with another girl. We weren't soliciting. We'd each had a high earlier, and had come down again, and we were wandering around because we just couldn't sleep.

Suddenly a pair of bobbies jumped out in front of us. It gave us quite a fright. But I wasn't worried. I knew I was clean. I'd taken all my pills earlier.

One of the policemen was a huge guy, tall and broad. He called me to one side.

'What's your name?' he asked.

'Audrey,' I said. 'Audrey Wilbraham.'

He looked down at me from what seemed like a great

height. 'Audrey, you don't belong on the street.'

I looked at him a bit surprised. Most of the policemen who stopped us young junkies gave us a cuff around the ear and told us to get lost.

I said to him: 'What do you mean?'

'You just don't belong on the streets. Listen, just keep yourself out of trouble for the rest of the night and I'll take you home when my shift is finished.'

He put his hand into his pocket and gave me a couple of pounds. 'Get yourself something to eat,' he said. 'Meet me outside West End Central station at seven o'clock.'

I can't remember what happened to my friend, but I lost her somewhere. I went to an all-night café and bought myself a hamburger and chips with the money the policeman had given to me. As I ate it, I was thinking to myself: 'I wonder what his game is? Does he want sex with me—or what?'

It wouldn't have bothered me too much if that was what he was after, although it had never happened with a policeman before. Not in uniform, anyway. I had two choices—I could scarper, or I could wait and see.

I decided on the latter. At seven I was waiting outside the police station, and he picked me up in his battered old car. He told me his name was Chris, and he drove me to his home in the East End. I was amazed when I met his wife, Ann. She was a tiny little lady just over five feet, and he was well over six feet.

Chris introduced me: 'This is Audrey. I think she could do with some breakfast and a rest.'

Ann was fabulous. First of all she showed me to the bathroom, and I had a lovely warm soak. Then she showed me to a bedroom, but before I went to bed she took me downstairs for some breakfast.

We were all chatting while we ate, and I told them I was on drugs which I'm sure Chris knew anyway. But I was still puzzled why he had brought me to his home, so I asked him.

He put down his knife and fork and looked at me. 'I did it because I am a Christian, and God asked me to speak to you last night. You can stay with us until you sort yourself out.'

I stayed with Chris and his wife for five days, but sadly I didn't sort myself out. At the first opportunity I was out on the street looking for someone to sell me some pills. Soon I was popping amphetamines like mad. I just couldn't manage without them.

I told Chris about my spot of bother down in Southend. He asked me if I had paid the fine after appearing before the magistrates. When I told him I hadn't, I could see he was worried.

'That's serious,' he said. 'It's only a small fine, but you could get arrested and put inside for not paying it. That's the sort of thing courts don't like.'

I gave him the date I had appeared in court, and he got on the phone to Southend. It seemed they were just issuing a warrant for my arrest. But they said they would drop it if the fine was paid right away. Chris wrote out a cheque for £10 and posted it off that day.

I had never encountered genuine goodness like this before, and I kept asking myself: 'What's their angle?' I couldn't understand it. Their whole attitude to life and people was something I just couldn't understand.

I didn't understand it, but I liked it. Here was somebody not just spouting from a pulpit, but living his Christianity. I couldn't appreciate exactly what it meant, but I admired them. They were two people living a life that was very very lovely.

I suppose this was the first time I had seen God's love in action. It spoke a lot more powerfully than a lot of sermons I've heard since. Chris said God would speak to me if I was prepared to listen. But I was dismissive. Why should God speak to me? Why should God bother with someone who had signed up with Satan?

Looking back on this encounter, I realise it would have been the perfect opportunity to break away from the coven. Chris and Ann were both strong in their faith, and they could have helped me, and protected me. But I didn't give them the opportunity.

After five blissful days, I told them I must go. The magnetic pull of the drug scene was too powerful for me to resist, and we parted.

It had been several months since I had had anything to do with the coven. Many times I had heard a buzzing in my head—Satan's telephone to let me know I was wanted. But I had ignored it. I assumed he didn't want his dancing partner too badly, otherwise he would have been more persistent.

Somehow the idea came into my mind, no doubt implanted by Satan, that the coven might help me get the drugs I craved. Perhaps this was his way of getting me away from the Christian influence of Chris and Ann.

So it wasn't long before I found myself on that familiar train to Virginia Water, heading for a meeting with my fellow witches.

When I rang Diana, she had told me when the meeting was. Even though it was six months or more since I had last attended a meeting, nobody batted an eyelid. Diana had said, 'We knew you'd be back,' and I was handed my robe and took my place in the circle without anyone saying a word.

It was a straightforward meeting of instruction and Satan worship without anything special. But afterwards I decided to have a word with the warlock. I suspect that he knew about the baby and my spell in hospital, but he didn't say anything about it.

What I wanted was money for drugs. At this time I always wanted money for drugs. I just couldn't get enough, and I thought the coven might be an untapped source. The warlock didn't offer me any money. But he did look very closely into my eyes, which must have been bloodshot and not a pretty sight. He said to me: 'You're taking drugs.'

I told him that I was needing them more and more, and I needed money to pay for them, and I was in a mess. He said: 'As long as you keep coming here, and working for us, we will provide drugs for you.'

He gave me a small sachet of white powder. It looked like talc, but it was heroin. I had taken most other drugs before, but never heroin.

I wasn't sure how to take it, so I took it like snuff, placing the powder in small piles on the back of my hand and sniffing it up each nostril.

I wasted a lot of that first dose. Sniffing an expensive drug like heroin was not the most economical way of utilising it. But I soon learnt. My pals around the Dilly were ready with their advice by the time I had been to another coven meeting, and received my second allocation.

The sort of quantities the warlock was giving me— enough for a couple of fixes—would have cost about £80 on the street, roughly £40 a shot.

Sniffing that first dose had made me sick, violently sick. So my friends told me to skin pop the next lot. Skin-popping is injecting the drug with a short hypodermic needle so that it lies just under the skin, and it is slowly absorbed into the bloodstream. This is quite different from mainlining heroin when you are craving large doses and you inject it into a vein. Mainlining was what I graduated to later.

My pals showed me all the tricks, usually in the toilets at Piccadilly underground station. That was a notorious hangout for junkies, and registered addicts went straight to these toilets after getting their legitimate prescribed dose from the all-night chemist.

The first thing they showed me was to take a tiny quantity of the powder and add water to it, usually scooped from the lavatory basin. Then we would cook it to dissolve it, holding a lighter flame or striking matches under a spoon. A few seconds of this heat was enough to make the powder vanish into the liquid. Then it would be drawn into the syringe ready to inject.

After I started mainlining, I was shown how to tie off – bind a tourniquet around my arm to restrict the blood flow causing the veins to bulge. The heroin was injected straight into the vein.

My main tutor was a girl called Betty. She was a regis- tered addict. But she could never get enough on pre- scription, so I shared some of the heroin the warlock gave me with her. She died later from an overdose.

We all shared our supplies, not because we were generous but for a practical advantage. If you carried heroin around with you, there was always the chance that you would be picked up by the police and they would search you and find it. But if you had enough for two fixes, which is the amount I was usually given, and you gave half to a friend, you weren't carrying anything for the police to find.

You could always claim it back when you needed it. You had to be able to trust your friends to repay you. Fortunately, even in that seamy society, there was trust, and I cannot recall a single occasion when somebody let a fellow addict down.

My addiction to heroin meant I needed the coven more than ever. I had tried to get away from them at the time I had the baby, and later when I went to Southend. But now I needed them, because they meant a regular supply of that white powder that had become a part of my life that I could not do without. Every three weeks when I went to coven meetings, the warlock renewed my supplies. It ensured him of my loyalty, and it ensured me of the regular fixes that my body screamed for.

I didn't always have to go to meetings to get my supply. If I needed heroin in between coven meetings, I had only to make a telephone call and a small parcel would be left, addressed to Luci, at the pub I used. This was usually just a small quantity—enough to tide me over until the next meeting. Then they could be sure I would attend.

The quantities the warlock handed to me went up, and up, as my needs increased. It must have been costing them thousands of pounds. But the coven was wealthy.

They must have thought I was worth it. Even though I was a relatively unimportant member, I was doing work for them, such as meeting young people at railway stations and bringing them to parties, which, as a young member, I could do better than any of the older witches.

Many of them were runaways with nobody to meet and nowhere to go, and these were the ones I tried to find. There was competition. The pimps were looking for them as well, talent spotting for trainee prostitutes.

I would go up to them and say: 'Hey, you look a bit lost.'

'Yes, I am,' they would answer, innocently.

'Would you like to go to a party tonight? There'll be plenty to eat and drink, and music, and you'll make some friends. You'll probably be able to get fixed up with somewhere to stay, as well.'

The response was almost always an eager acceptance. I'd give them the address, tell them what time to be there, and nine times out of ten they would turn up to be launched into their new career.

In all of this, my role was simply recruiting officer. I was pretty disgusted with what I was doing, because I knew the purpose. Those youngsters would be sent on a high on heroin vapour from the candles, and encouraged to take their clothes off and play about with each other.

Then they would be passed on to the evil men who wanted teenage boys and girls for sex. Many of them would be cast aside after their patrons tired of them, and they would finish up as young prostitutes.

As well as the parties, which were held every two or three months at different addresses, usually in North London, I witnessed one more meeting where young children were abused. It was the same sickening procedure as before, with a dozen youngsters, some almost babes in arms, being mauled and touched by those awful perverts—for money.

This was the money that was paying for the drugs that brought me a sort of artificial contentment. Now I hate even to think about it but then, as a follower of Satan, my conscience was seared to the evil of it all.

As well as blurring my thinking, the increasingly large doses of heroin I was taking had other effects. I began to neglect myself, going around unkempt and dirty. As for food, I just wasn't interested. Days and days went by without eating a single thing. There was simply no appetite. My only hunger was for more heroin. Occasionally someone would shove a hot dog under my nose, and I might eat it, but more often than not I didn't. My weight, usually just under ten stone, had gone right down to less than seven.

I ask myself now what the heroin did for me, and I have to answer: very little. The high that came after the injection, especially after I started mainlining, was a sort of bliss, that lasted for three or four hours. It took me out of myself, and left me floating above a troubled world that I was no part of. But when it wears off, you come down with a bump. Then you start looking around for the next dose, and the next trip.

The more you take, the shorter the span is. That is when you can overdose. A couple of times I overdosed, not deliberately but because I took the next fix while there was still heroin in my system from the last. It takes a while for the residue to flush out of your body, yet the mind can be asking for the next injection. It's a horrible vicious circle. Once you are in it, you can't see a way out.

In my more lucid moments, which came from time to time, I would say to myself: 'Right Audrey, that's it. No more drugs. You don't need them. You can do without them.' But I was kidding myself. At the first twinges of cold turkey, after I'd fought it for a while, I'd be off in search of the next fix. (Cold turkey is the awful hurtful shuddering that wracks the body with every organ screaming out for pain-suppressing heroin. Not pleasant.)

My main purpose in going to meetings of the coven was to pick up my supply of drugs, always handed to me by the warlock at the end of the session in a neat little sachet. The other business of the coven, the witchcraft, the actual worship of Satan, now took second place. But the dark knowledge I had assimilated was still there, and I could use it.

I once used it to put a curse on a woman who had upset me. I was in a shop, and there was a handbag on the counter. Nobody was looking, so I furtively opened it and snatched some money, about five pounds I think. But I had been spotted, and the woman chased after me. She caught up with me in the street, and recognised me. She was related to one of the barmaids who worked in the pub we used. She accused me of taking her money and threatened to call the police.

I managed to get away, but I was worried that she might go to the police. The young thieves who hung around the Dilly were well-known, and she had only to give a description of me and I was sure to be picked up. With my criminal record, I was afraid I would be sent to prison. Even if I was fined, I couldn't afford to pay it.

At that time I was using Molly's flat. I went back there, got hold of a piece of chalk and drew a pentagram on the floor. I drew an effigy in the middle, like a voodoo doll, and pushed a pin through the abdomen. I heard later that the woman who chased me was pregnant, and had lost her baby the day after. She probably thought it was running through the streets that had brought on a miscarriage, but I knew differently.

I once saw the warlock's powers used in a more dramatic way—the curse of death. There was a young man called Peter. He wasn't a member of our coven, which was all-female apart from the warlock, nor any of the covens we regularly met up with, but he had attended the satanic temple as a special guest.

This fellow Peter, it seemed, had been shooting his mouth off about the satanic temple and the evil things he had witnessed there. He wasn't trying to get us, or anybody else, into trouble. He was just a boastful young man who was trying to impress people with his scant knowledge of the occult, and trying to frighten them by claiming he had powers bestowed upon him by Satan.

I think the reason the witches were worried was that Peter spent quite a lot of time hanging around with us junkies in the West End. Often undercover policemen would try to infiltrate our group to find where we were getting our drugs from. They stood out a mile with their polished shoes and clean finger nails. We'd nudge each other and chuckle and be careful what we said. But Peter was such a big mouth some of the coven were frightened he would let something important slip out.

Our warlock got to hear of this wild braggart. He decided that this young man couldn't be trusted, and that his indiscreet talk could be dangerous. So the curse of death was put on him. This was unusual. More frequently a lesser curse would be put on people so that they would have some illness, or other misfortune. But

Peter, it seemed, had been warned previously about his wagging tongue, and had failed to heed the warnings. So it was decreed that he should die.

I saw it happen, along with many other people. We had been sitting in a café one morning, drinking coffee. Peter had been with us. Then he got up to leave. He walked outside and collapsed on to the pavement. An ambulance came but he was dead before they could get him to hospital.

His death was put down to a heart attack. But he was only twenty-two and a perfectly fit young man. I knew, and other members of the coven knew, that it was the curse that killed him. Satan is a powerful enemy, and if our warlock wished illness or death upon some adversary, Satan, if he could be persuaded that it was in his interest, invariably carried out that wish.

A coven and a satanic temple are similar, but there are technical differences. The coven tends to be more secretive, more protective, more cautious about who they invite to join them, and then they are attended only by members who have been initiated. The satanic temple is more open. They often have a building where meetings are held regularly. They hold masses at the temples, using the satanic bible, and they have a form of communion. But at both covens and temples, the main objective is to worship Satan.

Events like Peter's untimely death, which demonstrated Satan's powers so dramatically, filled me with a sort of admiration, and yet foreboding. I had to admire the strength of the power. After all, it was a hunger for this sort of power that had led me into witchcraft in the first place. But I was also dismayed, and a little frightened. If the warlock could bring about a remote control death sentence on a young man who simply talked too much, what might he do to me if I ever tried to leave the coven with the information I had?

Whenever I thought about this, it made me break out into a cold sweat and shake with terror. I was trapped. There was no escape. So I tried not to think about it. Or if I did, I found release, albeit temporary, with a spoonful of white powder, a flame and a needle.

9

Unholy Communion

As a witch, I did many deeds which now fill me with a bitter shame. But at the time, as a daughter of Satan, I performed some of these actions willingly—even with relish. I hate to say it, but some of them actually gave me a feeling of euphoria, almost the same sort of high you get by taking drugs.

Our evil midnight missions to desecrate churches I put into this category. The things we did in some of those churches were dirty and disgusting, but I invariably came away with a feeling of elation.

Much of my story is far from pretty reading, and what I'm going to relate in this chapter may be particularly upsetting to Christian readers. Yet it is important that Christian leaders, and those who pray, know what kind of mentality they are dealing with in the spiritual battle they have with Satan's forces.

Our objective when we set out to visit a church was not to destroy it, as vandals might, but to defile anything and everything that represented Christianity, and to show that our master, Satan, was more powerful than Christ. During my five years in the coven, we must have attacked eight or nine churches every year in London and the surrounding countryside, especially in Surrey and Sussex.

Usually we picked on churches in small villages, and

there was a second and more important reason than the obvious one that, because of their isolation, we were less likely to be disturbed in our long rituals. Older village churches are often built on the sites of pagan burial grounds, and this, to a Satan worshipper, gives an additional dimension to a raid. We felt closer to our master in such an environment with its history of supernatural observance. There were forces still lurking there from pre-Christian times that we could call up in our rituals.

I had no idea what was happening the first time I went on a church raiding party. It was in my early days as a witch, and I thought it was an ordinary meeting of the coven I had been summoned to at Virginia Water.

When we had all gathered in our usual meeting place, the bungalow, I noticed that we had been joined by members of another coven so I guessed something out of the ordinary was afoot. The warlock said something about visiting a church but I still didn't know what was going to happen. Then we all piled into cars and the convoy set off into the night.

I found myself sitting next to Mary, the girl whose baby was sacrificed at the first ever coven I attended on the night of my initiation. She looked pale and pensive. I thought I'd try to cheer her up.

'Are you missing the baby, love?' I asked.

She didn't reply. She smiled at me, acknowledging my question, but she didn't answer it. I suppose she was just too scared.

There must have been about half-a-dozen cars in the convoy heading along the dark roads. I've no idea which direction we took, but we had been driving for about ten to fifteen minutes before we pulled up in a lane alongside a village church. The locals must all have been asleep, otherwise, in the thin light of the moon, they would have seen a strange congregation making its way to the church doors that night.

We made no attempt to flit through the shadows. The robed figures boldly walked in twos and threes through the lychgate and up the path to the porch like Sunday morning churchgoers. We waited there to be led inside by the warlock.

The door creaked open and we witches, black cloaks making us almost invisible in the darkness, silently filed inside. I half expected the proceedings to take place in darkness. But no. Our leaders were quite brazen. They switched on a light.

It was a small church with wooden pews. The warlock led the group, about twenty-five of us, up the aisle to the altar rail. We stood there but he went on and stood before the altar in the place a priest would stand to conduct a service.

The first thing that he did was to remove the two white candles on either side of the altar and replace them with black candles. Then he took down the cross and laid it upside down on the floor.

The witches were quietly chanting. Though I didn't know the words, I found myself joining it. It was a rhythmic sound, semi-hypnotic. Then the warlock motioned us to stand in a line along the altar rail just like churchgoers waiting for the priest to dispense the bread and wine representing the body and blood of Christ in a Holy Communion service.

What happened next took me by surprise. I had seen some diabolical acts in my short career as a witch, but I was still capable of being shocked. And what I was seeing shook me to my toenails.

The warlock took the communion chalice and urinated in it. Then he brought the cross down and laid it just in front of the altar rail, still in the upside down position.

The first witch in the line stepped forward, spat at the cross, then knelt and took a sip from the chalice.

I watched in a daze until my turn came. Somebody nudged me and I went forward. I spat at the cross but nothing came out of my mouth. It was dry with fear.

Then I knelt at the rail. The warlock offered me a plate. I couldn't see in the dim light what was on it, but I picked it up and put it in my mouth. It was faeces. We were eating faeces and drinking urine in a horrible mockery of the Christian communion service.

It made me feel sick, but I managed somehow to stop myself vomiting. Not that it would have mattered. I discovered later that many of the witches forced themselves to vomit over the cross and elsewhere in the church, to add to the profanity.

After we had all taken part in this vile ritual, there was a further shock in store for me.

A young girl—she cannot have been more than twenty—was among the guests that night. I had noticed her earlier. She had a striking youthful complexion, fresh and innocent, which I found unusual in an apprentice witch.

That night in the church she completed her apprenticeship. Her robe and clothes were taken from her by other witches until she stood naked, her beautifully shaped body gleaming white in the dim light. Then she was led to the cross.

She was made to lie down on the cross which she did without protest. The warlock quickly stripped, lay on her and raped her.

Rape, perhaps, is too strong a word. She didn't struggle or protest. But she certainly didn't look as if she was enjoying the experience. Her eyes gaped wide in fear until the warlock had gratified himself. He grabbed her by the hair, yanked her roughly to her feet, and tossed her to one side. All she was to him was a prop to be used as another bit of the hideous ritual.

The purpose of that rape was, I believe, largely symbolic, a satanic rite to challenge God in this holy place where the village Christians gathered every Sunday, and to mock their faith.

I was standing quite close to the warlock while it happened. Again I was conscious of his acrid smell.

In witchcraft, or 'the craft' as we called it, so much happens in such a short space of time it's almost impossible to take it all in. The other witches had been on church raids before and were used to the drill. But these horrors piling on horrors left me reeling. I couldn't observe it all. I felt like a zombie.

After the rape, the proceedings developed into a free-for-all. I can't recall the warlock giving a signal, but all the witches suddenly began to do their own thing.

Diana went up to the lectern and began tearing pages out of the Bible, screwing them up and throwing them on to the floor. Another witch pulled down banners that were lining the walls, stamped on them and tried to rip them. Another began to smash up the white candles and grind them with her shoe into the floor.

Wherever I looked, vile scenes were being enacted. More defecation, more destruction and perverse behaviour. And all the time the witches were chanting. It was that same rhythmic chant. Somehow it seemed to have the power to drive them on. Everywhere in that church some despicable activity was in progress.

Suddenly I felt a nudge and a book was thrust into my hand. It was Mary who had given it to me. 'Come on, Luci,' she said. 'You'd better do your bit or Satan's not going to be too happy with you.'

The book she had given me was a prayer book. Grinning, she was ripping the pages out of the one she held, and she motioned me to do the same.

For a moment I couldn't. The memories came flooding back of that other prayer book I had once possessed— the one I had been given when I was confirmed, and which had been taken from me as a punishment by the matron at Dr Barnardo's.

Mary gave another nudge. 'Come on.'

I felt numb. But then, like a robot, I imitated her. I began to rip the pages from the book, one by one, screwing them up and letting them fall to the floor. I started doing it faster and faster.

Mary and I were having a race to see who could rip up the most pages. I suddenly realised I was enjoying it. Satan would have been pleased with the performance of his dancing partner that night, and he was making me feel happy and excited.

How long we spent in that church I do not know. It must have been an hour, possibly two. At the end of it, I was amazed at the feeling of bliss and contentment within me.

In spite of the horrible things we were doing, there was a strange sort of reverence about it all – reverence for Satan, our master. It was not wanton destruction. It was all done to show our allegiance to him. He would be pleased with our night's work – and it was important to please him.

In that brainwashed state, I felt that what I was doing, what we were all doing, was right. That church was occupied by Christ, but in pagan times the site would have been used by pagan worshippers. I felt it was right to drive out Christ, and restore to Satan what had been his.

When our work was completed, there was a final act to

show our hostility to the Christians. The warlock picked up the cross, held it above his head and, with all his strength, dashed it to the stone floor. It would not shatter, but it was dented – a permanent reminder to the worshippers of our visit.

We left the church quietly, switching off the light and closing the door behind us. I was driven back to Virginia Water and dropped off at the railway station to catch a train back to London.

Again I travelled with Mary. She seemed much happier than on the journey to the church. In fact she had an ecstatic look on her face. The exhilaration of the desecration mission had got through to her, as it had to me.

Mary and I were about the same age. She was the member of the coven I was closest to. Several times she seemed on the verge of talking to me, sharing her inner thoughts. But she always clammed up at the last moment, silenced by fear.

I was made out of different material—not so timid and more outspoken. But I also knew that fear. It kept me silent, too, but I would have liked a heart-to-heart with Mary.

Our roles in the coven were much the same. We were the brood mares. Mary had produced a baby to be sacrificed, and I am sure the baby the warlock fathered with me would have been destined to the same fate if I hadn't given it away.

As I waited for my train, the thought that kept coming back to me was ripping up that prayer book. Again I remembered my anguish when mine had been taken from me. Now I had destroyed somebody else's—and I'd enjoyed doing it.

That could only happen if I had become a true follower of Satan. I realised I had. I was as enthusiastic in my admiration for the devil as any other witch in that coven.

But that enthusiasm was soon to be put to the test. And it was found to be wanting. There were terrible things other members of the coven were happy to do. But I couldn't—never. These were when we became involved with the paedophiles who abused young children.

That happened more than once when we raided churches. Youngsters, who were drugged so they wouldn't make a noise, were brought along and used in hideous ceremonies to show our reverence for Satan.

I remember a little boy, who cannot have been more than six or seven, being tied naked to the inverted cross in one church and, while the circle of witches chanted, some of the men who had come along sexually abused that youngster.

I tried to hide when these awful things were going on. I'd dodge behind the lectern, or find a pillar to hide behind so that I couldn't see them. But I knew they were going on, and they sickened me. I love children. I always had. It upset me to see these terrible things being done to them.

If I knew children were going to be involved in any of the coven activities, I'd try to stay away. I found it too distressing to be there. But you had to come up with a good excuse if you had been summoned to a coven meeting, otherwise you could be in trouble. Serious trouble.

Twice I was beaten for not attending meetings. I was ordered to lie on the floor in front of the altar while the warlock thrashed me with a cane.

I had missed meetings when I was stoned on drugs, but for some reason I wasn't thrashed for that. Perhaps Satan, realising that his messages were not getting through to my befuddled brain, instructed the warlock not to punish me.

But I was determined to avoid going to one meeting where I knew children would be abused. An ordinary excuse I knew wouldn't wash—but they would have to accept my absence if it was for something serious like an illness that put me in hospital.

What I did was stupid and irrational but, as they say, seemed like a good idea at the time. I went into a toilet at Charing Cross with a bottle of coke and a needle. An assistant saw me and thought I was trying to overdose and called the police.

I was taken to St Thomas's Hospital. They didn't believe me at first when I told them I had swallowed a needle. But it showed up on an X-ray, and I was rushed into the operating theatre.

I still have the scars on my stomach where they opened me up to retrieve it. But it kept me away from a night at the coven where I would have had to witness again the dreadful things they did to youngsters.

There were many more raids on churches and, provided child abuse was not involved, I enjoyed them. They invariably gave me that feeling of exhilaration.

These raids varied in style. Sometimes we would hurriedly go into the church, knock over the cross, daub blood on the altar cloth and leave. It was like leaving a calling card, Satan's calling card, to say we'd been there, and might come back again.

Other times we would do a thorough job as on my first visit. But they didn't stick rigidly to a pattern. Sometimes we would have a blood sacrifice, a rabbit or a cockerel, and its blood would be mixed with the warlock's urine in the chalice for our unholy communion.

As well as our raids on churches, sometimes we went to satanic temples. The activities at these temples were quite different from the covens. The covens did more powerful and evil things. At the temples, they simply worshipped Satan as the son of God.

You may get as many as a hundred people at these temples. They really believe what they are doing. Everything is reversed from the Christian service. They even say the Lord's Prayer backwards, and use their own satanic bible.

Often I read in the newspapers about churches being attacked by mysterious people who smash stained-glass windows, tip up hassocks and daub slogans, including the 666 Antichrist's number on the walls. But these raids have nothing to do with witchcraft. They are committed by vandals, usually youngsters who get a thrill out of trying to imitate witches, and have no real supernatural significance.

Graveyards, too, are frequently attacked and headstones knocked over. Again, I believe it is vandals who are usually responsible. Real witches do not indulge in wanton destruction. Their evil deeds have much more depth and meaning.

We did, however, make use of graveyards, and I'm sure witches still do, for a purpose more sinister than silly vandalism. A grave is the perfect place to hide a body.

The baby who was sacrificed at my initiation ceremony was just nine days old, and all the evidence that it had ever lived, and of its awful death, was destroyed by burning the tiny body. But I had heard tales of older children, sometimes adults, being sacrificed. Their bones do not disintegrate so easily in a fire.

The favourite way of disposing of such bodies was in a graveyard. A grave would be carefully dug up and the coffin opened and the new body placed beside the mouldering corpse.

It's my belief that some of the hundreds of children and adults who go missing every year end up being sacrificed on the altars of the scores of covens which are flourishing today in English towns and cities. And

I'm sure that if the police were able to make a search of our graveyards, they would find many of those missing people sharing coffins with the official dead.

10

Nowhere Else to Go

The coven had introduced me to heroin not to do me any favours but to enslave me and make me a more willing servant of Satan. Yet, after I had been taking it for a few months, it backfired on them. I was too fuddled to be of any use to them. I had become so dependent on my regular fix that I couldn't be relied on to do the tasks they gave me.

The massive daily intake I now needed had other effects, too. Often I was so stupefied that I didn't hear Satan's call. He may have been shouting like mad, but when I was high on a heroin trip it fell on deaf ears, so his instructions to me were simply not obeyed.

The warlock, and the other members of the coven, must have known what they were doing when they handed out heroin to people like me. But they could not have guessed that I would become such a raving addict. I'm sure they didn't want to render their members impotent, but that is what I had become.

It had another effect. The coven had been my main source of supply—a free handout every time I went there. But I became so desperate that I needed a fix to get on the train to go there, and once I'd had that fix, I'd be off on a mental trip and I'd miss the train.

The long and short of all this was that I had to find other sources in London where I could obtain heroin without travelling. But that meant money, which was always in short supply.

A friend called Freddie came to the rescue. He was a cockney lad not much older than me. And he was an expert burglar who said he was prepared to teach me the tricks of his trade.

I don't think the house has been built that could keep Freddie out. He was magic. One short jemmy was the only tool he carried, and a tiny wire hook. He would jemmy a door at the locks, or bolts, and use the wire hook to slide back those burglar-proof chains so that they slipped out of the socket, allowing the door to swing open.

Once inside, he always knew exactly where to go. Wherever people hid their valuables, Freddie would soon find them. He seemed to be able to sniff out jewellery or money in the most unlikely places. He rarely broke into a house and came away empty handed.

Freddie had been a cat burglar since he was twelve. Fagin would have been proud to have him in his gang. He never did an honest job. But he did get caught once or twice, and had spent some time in prison.

I won't say he taught me all he knew—that would have taken too long. But Freddie did teach me the rudiments. We would get on a tube in Central London and go out to districts like Balham or Dulwich. We'd stroll around until we spotted a likely house, then we'd watch it for a while to see if there were any signs of life.

Friday night was always the most productive night of the week. It's surprising how many people went out and left their homes empty and unguarded on Fridays. We'd go out at about nine or ten o'clock and by midnight we were back at the Dilly, usually with a pocketful of money.

My haul, of course, went on drugs. Freddie was more sensible. He wasn't an addict. In fact, any drugs that he got his hands on he used to sell for a good profit.

Before long, I was going out on my own. I had my own jemmy, an iron bar about a foot long flattened at one end to slide it into the door jamb or under a window. I used to carry it in a long pocket down the leg of my jeans.

One trick I learned was to aim for the teapot. It's surprising how many people kept their spare cash in a teapot. If there was an ornamental pot on a mantelpiece, or in a cabinet, I'd always make straight for it, and I scored a jackpot time after time. To me, £50 was a jackpot. That was the largest sum I ever found. Usually it was much less.

When I broke into a house and found whatever money I could, I always made for the kitchen before leaving. I don't know if it was the excitement, or what, but I found burgling hungry work. Out on the streets I rarely bothered to eat, but in these strange houses I always fancied a snack. So I invariably made for the fridge and grabbed a lump of cheese or a chicken leg.

I was never caught burgling, or shoplifting, or for any of my criminal activities except for the fiver I pinched from Southend. It's surprising, really, because there were so many coppers around the West End. I'm surprised I never ran into their arms after some of the stunts I used to pull.

A favourite ploy was to pull out my knife and threaten people. Most of the heroin addicts carried knives to protect their supplies in case other addicts, desperate for a fix, tried to jump them. Sometimes when I was short of money, I'd go prowling around the streets until I came across a likely target.

Usually, I'd try to beg some money from them: 'Got a quid for a hungry girl, love?' But if it was in a quiet alleyway and there was nobody about, I'd pull the knife out and threaten them. I never used the knife. The threat was enough to get them to hand over their purse or wallet.

It was risky. A shout or scream would almost certainly bring the law running. And even if they bumped into a policeman after I had gone and gave a description, people like me who had been hanging around the West End for a long time would soon be picked up. I never was.

By some quirk, I was never caught in any of my criminal activities. Burglary, shoplifting, soliciting – I could have been sent to prison if I had been caught at any of them. In fact, the only time I went to prison it was for something I didn't do.

One of the gang that I was involved with had stolen some prescription pads from a doctor's surgery so that he could forge the signature and get drugs at chemists' shops. It was something that happened quite often. I used forged prescriptions dozens of times. Lots of doctors were careless with their pads and it was the work of an instant to slip one into your pocket while his back was turned.

Somehow the police got on to this racket and rounded up a group of us. They were after the man who had stolen the pads, who was a pusher. They never got him but about a dozen of the people who had used the forged prescriptions were hauled before the magistrates.

I was among them but, quite honestly, I'd had nothing to do with it. I can't even remember what I was charged with. I wasn't taking much notice. I thought the magistrates would hear my denial and set me free.

You can imagine my surprise when they remanded me in custody for further enquiries to be made. The police took me to Holloway. All my pleas that I was innocent fell upon deaf ears. When those prison gates clanged behind me, I was terrified.

One of my great fears was of being attacked by lesbians. Even though I was brought up in a female environment, it had never happened. In the forces I had seen plenty of lesbians, and in the coven advances had been made by several witches whose preferences lay towards women. But I had always been able to keep them away.

I had heard awesome stories about women in jail, especially Holloway, and I was gripped by a shivering terror that if my fellow prisoners didn't try to rape me, the wardresses would.

While I had a shower, they took away my clothes which were pretty filthy, and gave me a skirt and blouse. Then I went for a medical. The doctor took one look at my arms and knew immediately I was a junkie. They were like pin cushions. So he sent me to the prison hospital.

There was no treatment, no medication. I think they put me in the hospital just to keep me out of the way. Heroin addicts can be difficult when the drug is suddenly withdrawn from them. But my withdrawal symptoms were not too bad.

I had suffered cold turkey before: blinding headaches and agonising stomach cramps, sweaty and feverish, every muscle crying out in pain.

I was lucky. During those seven days in that prison hospital, my symptoms were only slight. I could cope with them. But I didn't like being in prison. I thought I'd kill myself rather than serve a long sentence.

At the end of a week, I was released. A police officer told me the case against me had been dropped. I didn't even have to go back to court. They simply opened the gates and let me go.

In a way I suppose that little spell inside was a comeuppance for all the things I'd done and got away with. I wasn't happy about it. But what legal redress was there for a penniless junkie? The very idea of me suing the police for wrongful arrest was laughable.

Prison did not diminish my need for heroin. When I walked out of Holloway, I was desperate for a fix. I went straight back to my West End haunts to arrange one.

The heroin the warlock supplied me with was pure, top quality stuff. But when I had to rely on pushers around the streets, I was often cheated. They would mix it with baking powder, or flour, to make you think you were getting more for your money. You wouldn't know if it had been diluted – it was just that your high didn't last so long.

The street dealers were charging up to £40 a fix, and by this time I was taking three fixes a day. There were other sources such as my cronies who were registered addicts. Sometimes I was able to buy, or borrow, half their prescribed dose, and this would be much cheaper. I could often pick up a fix for a couple of quid. I've even known registered addicts to sell their prescription when they felt they needed money more than the drug.

Most of the time at this period I was either on a high, or recovering from one, or getting some money together to pay for the next. It's hard to describe to someone who has never taken drugs the effect of heroin. Usually it gives you a blissful floating feeling, taking you away from the world and its problems.

But there were bad trips as well, when you would have the most terrifying hallucinations. I remember having one bad one when there were maggots, millions of them, crawling up a wall and falling on to me and wriggling all over me. A trip like that would leave me a shuddering wreck.

From time to time I called at the pub we used off Curzon Street. By now, the small parcels of heroin addressed to Luci had stopped. It made me think, in my rare lucid moments, that the coven had finished with me, given me up as a bad job. The coven wanted on-the-ball witches with clear minds and powerful concentration. By their standards, a junkie with her mind blown by drugs was a pretty useless proposition.

I was quite pleased to be rid of them, and not to have Satan's voice calling me. I had long given up any hope of achieving real power and wealth like some of the other witches. If they had decided to let me go, I was quite happy about it. I certainly wasn't going to go looking for them.

It occurred to me, again in those infrequent periods when my mind was working properly, that the coven might not be so happy. Losing recruits was not something they relished. I had never seen them mete out any punishment to a deserter, but I had seen the effects of their power on other people they wished to harm. And I worried that they might try to get me, either physically or by using Satan.

Usually, when a coven puts a death curse on someone, that person is informed. The knowledge that it is there causes fear, and makes the curse more effective. But I knew they had the power to put a curse on somebody without the victim knowing anything at all about it. They would just die in an accident, or from a heart attack like Peter.

Sometimes, I thought I had been cursed. Some of my trips on heroin were so bad, leaving me feeling so ill, I felt some force must be working against me. Twice I accidentally took overdoses in the frenzied rush to get a needle into my arm. These so-called accidents could easily have been arranged by the coven. How could I ever know?

One of the places we used to go to was a place run by the Salvation Army in Soho. It was modelled on night club lines with a bar and chairs and tables, but the bar did not serve hard liquor, of course—just tea, coffee and soft drinks.

The captain there was a kind young man. When we

were broke and hungry, he often forgot to charge us for a meal. It was open through the night and there was a strict rule about no sleeping, but when I was very tired he let me lie down on a bench and have a nap.

My stay with Chris the policeman served to show me how squalid my own lifestyle was compared with normal people, and I began to have chats with the Sally Army captain. I told him I was fed up with the way I was living and would love to change it but I didn't see how I could.

He listened intently. He was a good listener. He didn't preach to people unless they asked him to. But he would mull over any problems people took to him and quietly try to help.

When I told him I wanted to kick drugs, he said: 'Do you really mean it? If you're really sure, we might be able to help you.'

I talked to people, such as the captain and the policeman, about my drug taking. But I told nobody about my involvement with witchcraft. This was a dark secret I kept to myself. I felt that nobody would be able to help me. But at this time it wasn't a problem. I thought I had blotted it out and it would never come back.

The captain went on: 'God can give you a new life if you're genuinely looking for one. We can get you into a psychiatric hospital where they can help you get off drugs.'

In his typical quiet way, he went about making the arrangements. Two days later, he drove me to one of the big London hospitals and I was admitted into the psychiatric ward.

The doctor in charge told me they could help if I signed myself in. I had a bath and an examination. They quizzed me about what drugs I was taking. Then I was put into a bed.

They started a slow withdrawal from drugs. They put me on methadone, a substitute for heroin. The withdrawal was so gradual I didn't get the dreaded cold turkey. But even after a week, though my body wasn't craving drugs, my mind was.

I was in the hospital that unforgettable night in July, 1966, when England beat West Germany to win the World Cup. All the other patients were going barmy, shouting and cheering for England. The game went into extra time with England winning by four goals to two. I lay there glumly, not caring about the result, wishing they would all shut up and let me get some peace.

At the hospital they did their best for me. They trained my body to exist without its daily quota of heroin, but there was nothing there to fill my mind. It was a void, as if a chunk of my life had been cut away with a scalpel and nothing put back to replace it.

I lay in that bed, tossing and turning and craving a fix. But the doors were locked and I couldn't just go out and get one. I even thought if I could get in touch with the coven, perhaps Satan, if I begged hard enough, would arrange just one fix for me.

I was having visitors but I don't think they realised the mental torture I was going through. The Salvation Army captain and his wife came to see me. And Chris and Ann also came. Ann brought me a present – the first really pretty nightie I had ever had—red with little white frills.

At the hospital I began to feel like a woman again, instead of the scrap of dirt I had become. Ann bought talcum powder and nice smelling perfume. They washed, cut, and set my hair, getting rid of the lice. I could look into a mirror again without recoiling and think to myself: 'You're not bad looking.'

Unfortunately, I didn't see the course of treatment through. I should have stayed there at least three weeks, but after two-and-a-half weeks I couldn't stick another day. There was nothing they could do to keep me there. I had gone in as a voluntary patient—and now I volunteered to leave.

I behaved, I'm sorry to say, in my usual manner to the people who had tried to help me. I didn't tell them I was leaving. I just left—and I showed my gratitude by leaving the presents they had brought me in my hospital locker, including that lovely nightie.

My pals at the Dilly welcomed me back. I hadn't any money but there was no shortage of drugs. They are always ready to help someone who has tried to take a cure, and failed. They help them with a free fix. And after nearly three weeks off heroin, it only took a tiny dose to send me sky high.

Within days, I was back to the old routine. Days and nights blurred together in my continuous pursuit of drugs. I was in a state of limbo, never fully aware of what was going on. For all the good my hospital stay had done, I might never have been there.

There was one place in London where we used to get a welcome, in spite of our dirty clothes and unkempt appearance. There was a Congregational Church in Orange Street, just a short walk from the Dilly. They turned the basement into a coffee bar where drop-outs could get a free cup of coffee and a bun on a Sunday night.

Members of the church used to mingle with us and try to share their Christian beliefs. I remember one of them saying to me: 'You don't have to live this way. Jesus can save you from drugs. The power of God can change your life.'

They were kind, and they knew how to talk to young people without being patronising, or too forceful. I listened to bits of it. But I tended to think: 'It's all right for you. But you haven't been where I've been. You're not worried about where the next fix is coming from.'

They were loving, caring people, and I tried to listen to them. But I didn't really believe that they could help me. I thought my sins were too many and too bad for Jesus to bother with me, even though they patiently tried to explain that all sinners could be saved.

I kept going to that basement, but it was mainly for the coffee and buns. The people from the church tried to reach me—but I was still within Satan's grip, and an invisible barrier prevented their words getting inside me. They did manage to arouse my curiosity—something was kindled in that basement, but the spark never burst into flame.

There was one bright moment that still shines out with its warm humanity in that gloomy period of my life. It was the Christmas of 1966. It was one of the nicest Christmases I've ever spent. And it was Molly, my prostitute friend, who made it possible.

There were about eight of us junkies, all living rough, with nowhere to go and no prospect of a happy Christmas. Molly invited us all to use her flat, above a coffee shop looking down on to St Anne's Church in Dean Street, Soho.

She had decided she was going to take a holiday from business over Christmas, and had gone to her home in Ireland. Before she went she decorated the little flat with sprigs of holly. We took food, drink, cigarettes, fruit, whatever we could afford to buy—or steal. And we all settled down.

There were no drugs. Molly knew her flat was watched from time to time by vice squad police, and she did not want to be caught with drugs on the premises. We respected her wishes. If anyone needed a fix, they had to go outside for it.

On Christmas Eve we heard the church bells ringing and looked from the window down onto the church. People were going to the service. I stood gazing at them for a long, long time, wondering what they were getting from that service, and whether I could get the same. None of us went, but we all talked about it, and what we might have been doing that evening if circumstances had been different.

I said I didn't know where I would be, because I hadn't got a family. One of the lads said he would dearly love to be at home but he had been kicked out when his parents discovered he was a junkie. It was a bit morose as we shared our unhappy life stories, but we were warm and comfortable.

On Christmas Day the church bells rang out again. Once again we debated going to the service, but debate was as far as it got. I spent even longer at the window, waiting until the people came out. I could see their faces. They seemed serene, as if they had heard good news in that church.

If only I had been able to join them, how different my life would have been. If only I had stepped inside that church, or listened to the simple wisdom of the people in Orange Street. If only I knew then what I know now.

God would have protected me from Satan and the evil of the coven. Jesus would have banished the demons that were in possession of my soul. If only.

But it didn't happen. I felt a longing to go, but I didn't take that step. I suppose I didn't want to break up our cosy little group. And I think I was a little bit scared of the reaction of the other worshippers towards me. They were all dressed in their finery. All I had was a scruffy sweater and jeans.

I now know that those things are unimportant. A real Christian doesn't care what his fellow worshipper is wearing. I am sure if I had gone into St Anne's and joined in their Christmas service, I would have been warmly welcomed, and probably invited back to somebody's home for a slap-up Christmas dinner. Wouldn't I?

We talked and ate and drank and slept, and we all took turns to have a bath and wash our clothes, wearing towels and borrowed dressing gowns while they dried.

Curiously, even though we'd been looking down together at the church and the people going in and out, we didn't talk about our religious experiences. We talked about families, and past Christmases, but there seemed to be a strange reluctance to talk about our beliefs. It was as though we were holding back—too frightened to share in case we found ourselves wallowing in deep and embarrassing waters.

That is a lesson my faith in Christ has taught me. You can share it with anybody and everybody. There is no embarrassment. Alas at that time I didn't have the benefit of a strong faith.

Perhaps if Molly had been there, things might have been different. She was a devout Roman Catholic in spite of her profession. Who knows? She may have led us all to mass. She was a great girl, really kind. When I think back I can almost hear her lovely soft Southern Irish accent. She had a magnificent low throaty laugh. When she laughed, everybody else laughed with her. The kind-hearted whore might be a bit of a cliché, but in Molly's case it was for real.

After that Christmas, there seemed to be a huge emptiness in my life. It was all the talk in Molly's flat that brought it to the surface. We'd been talking about families, and I had an overwhelming desire to belong somewhere. But looking around, I had nothing, nobody.

It was then that I began to think of the coven. For weeks it had been out of my mind. But now I was telling myself: 'Audrey, that is the only family you are ever going to have.'

The thought repulsed me. Yet, who else was there? Who else wanted me? Where else did I belong?

These were the people I was most closely linked with, links forged by the vile things we had done together. I began to think there was no hope for me at all. I belonged to Satan. I always will belong to Satan. I'll end up dying for Satan. Full stop.

I found myself dwelling on these thoughts. Even the

drugs could not shift them. I had cut down my intake quite a bit since the spell in hospital. I didn't need as much.

And now the voice began to call in my head again. Satan was beckoning his dancing partner. There was no resistance. I had to go.

I knew there was a meeting of the coven. Nobody told me, but I knew. So I got on a train for Virginia Water. I cannot remember how I found my way—whether I was given a lift or took a taxi. But I ended up at the house where I had been initiated into the coven, and seen the baby sacrificed.

I went in and put on my robe and joined the witches who were already there. There was no welcome from them, no smiling faces, no communication, not even recognition.

The warlock cut the throat of a cockerel and passed around the chalice of blood. But when my turn came, the cup was not offered to me. He just swept past as if I wasn't there and handed the chalice to the witch on my right.

I realised then I was being squeezed out and that they didn't want me. Yet I wanted them, I needed them. They were my family, but they were casting me out.

Then the warlock brought out the parchment I had signed in my blood with the point of the athame. He didn't say anything. He just indicated the bloodmark below the words of my oath to Satan.

'I am no longer my own. Satan is my master. I live only to serve and honour him.'

They were squeezing me out. They were not including me in the rituals. Yet they were reminding me of my covenant with Satan. They were kicking me out—and telling me in the same breath I must not leave.

I felt like screaming: 'What am I to do? Please, somebody tell me.' But some inner voice was whispering to me that if I opened my mouth in protest, something terrible would happen to me.

11

Curse of the Coven

That night when I walked out of the coven, I knew it was for the last time. But it was the beginning of the worst night of my life. As I handed in my robe, I sensed the other witches knew I had decided never to return. It was this that worried me.

Would they let me get away from them? Or would they exact their revenge on a deserter, especially one who knew so much, by putting a curse on me?

As I walked along the dark roads on my way to the railway station, I kept looking over my shoulder. Was I being followed? Were those footsteps I could hear? I saw someone hiding in every shadow.

There were four or five hours to wait for the first train into London. I huddled on a bench on the station, but couldn't sleep. I kept thinking someone from the coven would creep up and stick a knife through me. Or perhaps they would call upon Satan to make me harm myself by walking under a train.

The more I thought about it, the more worried I became. No way were my satanic sisters going to let me walk out on them without taking any action to punish or silence me. But what could I do? How could I guard myself against their evil powers?

I thought of ringing the police but I knew they wouldn't believe me. Imagine the desk sergeant picking up the phone: 'What's that, luv? Who do you say is after you? A crowd of witches? Yes, yes. Go on. Pull the other one.'

Every movement, every sound in that gloomy station waiting room, had me sitting bolt upright and peering into the darkness. It was a long, long night. I don't think I've ever been so pleased to see a train arrive.

Back in London, I made straight for the Dilly for the fix I so badly needed. Luckily there were friends around, as there nearly always were, to see me all right.

It wasn't many days before something happened to remind me of my covenant with the devil. I accidentally took a drugs overdose. I was sure it was the usual amount of heroin I cooked up, and I'd had plenty of practice at squirting it into my arm. But something went wrong.

I passed out in the lavatories at Piccadilly and was discovered by the cleaner who called an ambulance. I came round in hospital. But I didn't stay there—I just waited until nobody was watching and simply walked out when I felt well enough after a few hours' rest.

The same thing happened a month later. This time I was with friends in a derelict house. As usual, I was careful with my dose. But I collapsed just after taking it, and again I came round in hospital.

The first time I didn't think too much about it. But the second was too much of a coincidence. I began to worry. Was this the coven's work? Was Satan there helping me judge the amount of heroin? Were they trying to get rid of me by making it look like an accidental overdose?

That is what I began to suspect. It certainly hadn't been intentional on my part to take more than my usual fix.

At the second hospital, a psychiatrist tried to persuade me to stay on and register for treatment. He said: 'The rate you're going, my girl, you'll be dead within six months. You can't carry on the way you are.'

I shrugged it off. I wasn't one to take advice—medical, moral, or any other sort. But it worried me a few weeks later when my friends began to get concerned. They were not the sort of people to worry about their own health, or that of their friends, otherwise they wouldn't have been living the lives they did. But every time I met them their eyes gaped open and they kept saying: 'Audrey, you look terrible.'

Once or twice I caught a glimpse of myself in a mirror. They were right. It got to the stage where I tried to stay away from mirrors. But from the odd glance I got of myself in shop windows, I could see that I was turning yellow. My face, the back of my hands, were all tinged with an awful deathly yellow hue, and the words of the doctor came ringing back.

My weight had shrunk from nine stone to under six. All the time I felt weak and listless. I couldn't sleep properly. And I knew who was behind it all—the coven. This was Satan attacking me. They had the power to kill me quickly, but they were tormenting me by organising a slow death. I wasn't going to put up with it any more.

It was strange. I had never felt like this before. But suddenly I wanted to fight Satan, and beat him. I was determined not to let him have his way by dying in the gutter like some diseased rat.

I didn't want to die at all—I wanted to beat him by staying alive. But, at least, if I was to die, I was going to make sure it wasn't a squalid backstreet death. I would die properly and with dignity in a clean bed, not in a cardboard box.

I had heard from friends of the drug rehabilitation centre at Tooting Bec Hospital, and I decided to give it a go. Previously, when I had tried to kick drugs, it was on the advice of other well-meaning people, and I had failed. But this time it was my decision. If I failed again, I would only be letting myself down.

So one morning I set out on the tube and turned up at the out-patients department at the hospital. The girl at the reception desk looked aghast at me. Yellow-skinned with matted hair and dirty clothes, I was not a pretty sight.

They realised that I was badly in need of treatment and, within an hour, I had been registered, bathed, examined and put into a bed in the sick ward on a drip feed. The doctors diagnosed I had a serious case of jaundice, quite a common illness for drug addicts whose livers are affected by the constant heavy barrage of heroin.

I was quite open with the doctor when he asked me what I had been taking. Heroin was just the last of a long list. When I reeled them off—cocaine, barbiturates, amphetamines, purple hearts, booze, anything I could get—he shook his head sadly and said: 'Quite a cocktail!'

The jaundice soon cleared up and, with treatment and proper food, I began to look better and put on weight. Once again they were treating my addiction by gradual withdrawal, giving me diminishing doses of heroin, or the substitute methadone. Slowly I began to feel human again. I felt as if I was winning.

One afternoon the nurse came to my bed. 'Hey, Audrey. You've got a visitor,' she said.

I was surprised. Only my junkie friends knew I was there. I didn't think it likely they would take the trouble to come to see me. They wouldn't be encouraged by the hospital authorities, anyway. There were seven or eight of us in that acute ward, but there were very few visitors. The only person I can remember visiting us was the hospital chaplain.

'Oh,' I said. 'I wonder who it can be.'

The nurse pumped up my pillow, sat me up and went away. For a few seconds I was alone. Then I became aware of a man standing at the foot of my bed. He was smartly dressed in a dark suit and carrying an umbrella. I didn't recognise him.

He didn't speak. He didn't smile. He just stood there gazing at me. There was something familiar about his eyes, but I still didn't recognise him.

The moment he opened his mouth and the first word tumbled out, I realised who he was. Without his hood masking part of his face, and in daylight instead of the semi-darkness of the black altar candles, he looked quite different. I recalled those eyes—black bottomless pits. It was the warlock, the man who had raped me, the man whom I had seen slit a baby's throat.

The fear started as a tingle in my toes and fingertips and spread throughout my body. What was he doing here? How had he found me? What was he going to do to me? Surely he couldn't hurt me in a hospital ward with doctors and nurses around.

His eyes transfixed me as he began to speak in that voice I had heard so often, a posh voice tinged with a slight upper-class cockney accent.

'Wherever you go, whatever you do, you will never, never have peace of mind. You have deserted us—and Satan will pursue you.'

That was all. Just a couple of simple sentences. But they are scorched on my memory like tyre tracks on virgin snow. I can hear them now, years later, as though they were uttered seconds ago.

Those few words were to echo and re-echo through my life, bringing torment and tragedy. The warlock had come to deliver the curse of the coven. When he had given me his message, he quickly wheeled round and was gone.

Nobody else in the ward realised what had happened. The nurses were going about their business. The girl who had announced my visitor came to my bed after a little while.

'Nice-looking man, your visitor. He didn't stay long, did he?'

'No.'

If they had only known that my nice, respectable visitor, looking like a favourite uncle with his grey sideburns, was an emissary of the devil! But there was nothing they could have done. There was nothing anybody could do. I had made my pact with Satan, and now I was to pay.

I must say that at the time I was not terribly bothered. I was too ill to worry overmuch about a curse. I couldn't forget it, but I put it to the back of my mind to concentrate on getting better.

After a month in the clinical ward, they moved me into the hospital proper. Tooting Bec is a psychiatric hospital, and I had the shock of my life when I was moved in with the other patients. They were a very strange lot—but then they probably thought that I was a bit odd, too.

Filling in the time was the problem once I began to get well again. They gave me a sketching pad and a set of paints, and I found drawing and painting helped me to relax. I had always been fond of art: I'll never be a Rembrandt or a Van Gogh but some of my efforts were quite creditable.

I soon learned that even in a psychiatric hospital where people went to be cured of drug addiction, drugs were available. I'm not talking about the prescribed drugs handed out by the doctors as part of the cure. Some of the patients smuggled in drugs, or got their visitors to bring them. Pretty well everything that was available on the street was available in that hospital ward.

I didn't shoot any heroin while I was there, although I was offered some and told that it was hidden in a plastic bag in the water cistern in one of the toilets. But I did take purple hearts from time to time.

It was not that my body was craving for drugs, but I

needed them simply to relieve the boredom. When doctors wean you off drugs, it leaves a vacuum in your life. Unless you can find something to fill it—and there's not much in hospitals—there's a great temptation to use drugs.

Each morning I woke up and the day stretched ahead of me like a void. I talked to the nurses about the problem to try to find something to do to pass the time. One of them mentioned a man called Frank Wilson who ran an organisation called Life for the World, set up to help drug addicts in London.

The nurse, a sweet caring girl whom I had come to like, said to me: 'Why don't you write to Frank Wilson? He does good work. He may be able to help you.'

She said that he was a reverend and I turned down the idea, saying I didn't want any help from reverends. But she mentioned it on a couple of other occasions.

One day she said: 'Why don't you write him a letter? I've got his address. I'll post it for you.'

'All right,' I said. 'I'll give it a whirl. Get me some paper.'

She produced a notebook, and I wrote:

Dear Rev,
  I have heard you help drug addicts. I'm told I'm beyond help but if you can spare time to say a prayer for me I would be grateful.
  Cheerio!
  Love, Audrey Wilbraham.

The nurse took the letter and I forgot all about it. I was more concerned with my boyfriend, a lad called Alan. He was an addict like myself, and he was in the hospital for a cure. But his home was just a short walk from the hospital, and he invited me there for weekends with his parents.

Those weekends were useful, because Alan's mother

had an endless supply of purple hearts. She used to get them from her doctor for depression, but Alan discovered where she hid them, and he kept me supplied.

We were all gathered around the TV set one afternoon watching some pop star singing when one of the patients shouted from the other end of the ward: 'Audrey, there's someone to see you.'

I was rolling a cigarette at the time, and the place was thick with smoke. I called back: 'Who is it?'

The voice of one of the older characters, a woman who had been in the hospital for years, came back: 'He says he's a reverend.'

I shouted back: 'I don't know any reverends.'

Through the clouds of tobacco smoke a large figure materialised. He said: 'Are you Audrey? I'm Frank Wilson.'

'Crikey, you've come!' I said. 'I never thought you would.'

I took him to a quiet corner of the ward and we sat down to talk. He was a brave man walking into that lot. He was big and handsome and all the women patients were taking the mickey, and calling out: 'You've got yourself a bit of all right there, Audrey. Lucky girl!'

I told him a little about my life, but I never mentioned the witchcraft. I didn't tell anybody about that. If it got back to the psychiatrists that I'd been talking about devil worship, I was afraid that they would think I had been hearing voices in my head and they would keep me in that hospital for ever. So I had to fight Satan on my own without any allies.

Frank Wilson was a good listener. He preached a little, but not too much. He told me God loved me, and could save me. He told me that if I put my faith in God, I wouldn't need to take drugs any more.

On that first visit, he stayed about an hour. He didn't overdo it, which was just as well because I didn't want him to. But I sensed that he wanted to help me, and had the ability to help me. He asked if he could call and see me again, and I said I would like him to.

Frank's visits became quite frequent. He would call about once a week. He talked to other patients as well. But he seemed to concentrate on me. Perhaps he had seen a glimmer of hope.

Even when I got to know Frank well, and I'd stayed with him and his family a few times, I never told him about my dalliance with Satan. By now I hardly ever thought of the coven. I thought I'd licked the problem and that it was a chapter of my life that had finally closed.

Frank invited me to spend a weekend with his wife, Shirley, and their two daughters at their home in Harrow. He drove down to Tooting Bec and picked me up. I went with some trepidation. Drug addicts are anti-social people, and I just didn't know how I'd fit into a civilised household.

I needn't have worried. Shirley was lovely, and I so enjoyed playing with their two girls. But I had this feeling that Frank might start preaching to me, and I knew I couldn't have coped with that. I wasn't ready for it.

Frank invited me a second time. But that visit didn't work out as planned. He couldn't pick me up, and I was travelling to Harrow by tube. I'd even paid for my ticket instead of bilking.

But I had to change trains at Charing Cross, and that was my undoing. The Bakerloo Line went right under Piccadilly Circus and the pull was just too much. I got off the train and, with mounting excitement, went up the escalator and out into the Dilly.

I wasn't going to have any drugs, of course. I'd beaten that. I was strong. I could resist it. The only reason I had come here, I told myself, was to look up old pals. But I was lying—even to myself.

Yes, I did meet old friends. 'Hey, it's Audrey!' a gang of them cried. One of them had some heroin. I went with her into the ladies' lavatory, tied up my arm and took a shot. I was high again, very high after such a long time without any. It went straight to my head, and I was vomiting all over the place.

Instead of spending the weekend at Frank Wilson's house, I was picked up by the police. When I'd recovered enough to tell them who I was, they got in touch with a social worker at Tooting Bec, confirmed that I was a patient there, and took me back to the hospital in a police car.

Frank was lovely when I rang him the next day to explain and apologise. He knew all about the urges heroin addicts experience. 'Never mind, Audrey,' he said. 'One of these days you'll be able to get across London and not be tempted.'

I had two or three lapses when I set out for Frank's house, and failed to arrive. He was a very understanding man, and never gave up on the young people he pledged to help.

I said to him: 'What you don't understand, Frank, is that because the drugs are there I will always be drawn there.'

It was Frank's dream to get a place in the country, an old mansion house well away from everywhere, where he could take addicts and keep them away from the temptations of the city scene. I'm glad to say that eventually he made it at Northwick Park (which he wrote about in his book *House of New Beginnings*). But for now Frank said, 'I don't have that place at the moment. You need somewhere away from London. Let me see if I can find someone who will take you.'

At that time the organisation that sponsored Frank's work, Life for the World, was planning a meeting in London, aimed at young drug addicts like myself. It was to be led by the Reverend Eric Hutchins at the Metropolitan Tabernacle on a Saturday night early in 1967. Frank asked me if I'd like to go.

I wasn't sure, but I knew he wanted me to, so I said I would. He arranged to pick me up and take me so I wouldn't fall by the wayside. On the way I was nervous. I remember cracking weak gags as we drove through Piccadilly Circus.

'Drop me off here, Frank. You can pick me up later. I want to pop into Boots for some talcum powder.'

Talcum powder was a little snatch of addict's slang for heroin. Frank wasn't taking any chances. He leaned over and locked the car door just in case I jumped out.

When we got to the Tab, as it is called, the place was packed. Eric Hutchins was a very popular evangelical preacher, and his crusades attracted vast crowds of people.

Frank had told me there would be addicts at the meeting who had managed to give up drugs and remain clean for years. This was the part that interested me. I truly wanted to do the same. If there was anything to be learned from the example of these people, I was ready to listen.

I was jittery. I had never been to a religious meeting before. I didn't quite know what to expect. The place was packed, and I chose a seat at the back. I wanted to be near the door in case I decided to make a bolt for it.

At the start it was a little bit boring. I was desperate for a fag, but I had to make do with a supply of mints I had brought. But my ears began to prick up when the young people at the front started standing up and giving their testimonies.

I was surprised by their appearance. They were dressed just like me. And they talked about how they had overcome their drug addiction after God had come into their lives.

One young man, just a couple of years younger than me, made a particular impact. He had been taking drugs since he was thirteen, he said, and mainlining heroin for a couple of years. He had been involved in violence, and had even been in prison.

He spoke gently and sincerely about his past, and said how it had all changed. Instead of being useless and empty, now he felt fulfilled and full of love. He had become reunited with the family who had thrown him out. And all of this had happened after he had invited Jesus into his life.

These were people I could identify with. They were ordinary, and they spoke in plain down-to-earth language about their experiences. As I listened to them, I suddenly realised my yearning for a cigarette had gone.

People then stood up to sing a hymn, 'Oh the deep deep love of Jesus.' I couldn't sing it that night, as I didn't know the words or the music, but it has since become a favourite for me.

Eric Hutchins stood up to preach. I can't remember his text, but his words were delivered with a quiet gentle authority. I found him a gripping preacher, and I leaned forward to concentrate on his message.

It was aimed at the sinners and junkies in the congregation. But he wasn't castigating us. He was saying we could be helped.

'Jesus didn't die for perfect people, but for sinners,' he said.

'That's good,' I thought. 'That's me.'

'No matter how far down in the gutter you are, Jesus can reach you,' he said.

'He's got a long way to reach me!' I thought.

He told us about the crucifixion, and how Jesus had listened to the plea from the thief on the cross by his side. I had heard these stories before when I was in Dr Barnardo's, but Eric Hutchins had a way of bringing

Christ to life and presenting us with a real person, relevant to our lives now.

He said that if we asked Jesus Christ he would put his Spirit in us to make us strong, so that we were able to resist temptation. I listened because I was interested, and I certainly wanted to kick drugs. But I didn't know whether to believe it or not.

There was something Eric Hutchins and Frank and every other preacher said that I just couldn't come to terms with. They all talked about the God who loves everybody.

But if God loved me, why was my life so squalid? Why couldn't I have a home? Why couldn't I have a family like other people? There were still a lot of questions—and a lot of conflict.

I had this longing for a better life, but I just didn't seem to be able to achieve it. God forgives everybody, they were saying. Great. But would he forgive me after my little affair with Satan?

All these thoughts were going through my mind at that meeting. We were being asked to respond to the gospel.

I thought: 'If this God will forgive me and pick me up out of the gutter and give me a better life, all right then, I'll give it a go. If it doesn't work, I'm no worse off.'

I was uttering my own little prayer, unbeknown to the rest of that congregation. 'God, if you're there, you save me. If you really love me, you show me that you love me. If you really are who these people say you are, then you show me a new life.'

It was really not a very nice way to put it, I suppose, but I felt a little seed of hope take root inside me. Maybe, just maybe, God could work out all this mess and make me feel clean again. I'd got nothing to lose.

I continued with my prayer. I said, 'All right then, God. This is Audrey speaking. You have me. Go on, take me, all of me, rotten bits and all. And you show me that you love me.'

I noticed a lot of people, including Frank, were quite weepy by the end of the meeting, and I was surprised to find I was as well. Eric Hutchins had spoken beautifully about what God could do for people, and I thought that was what I wanted, to feel clean and forgiven.

I still felt tainted by the coven. I wasn't pure, I wasn't clean, I wasn't lovely—but I wanted to be all these things.

All the members of the congregation who wanted to accept God into their lives were asked to step to the front. I wasn't sure, but I went. I cannot say that I felt a sudden dramatic change in my life. But there was a glow of hope that I hadn't felt earlier.

I went back to the hospital on Cloud Nine. All that love at the meeting gave me a sensation of floating. I'd told God what I wanted, and if he was as powerful as the preacher said, I could now look forward to something good in my life. I expected God to sort out all my problems, and to wake up in the morning a different person with no need for drugs.

I realised later I hadn't given a thought to Satan, or the terrors of the coven, that night at the Tab. They were completely out of my mind, as if I had escaped for ever. I felt free of the curse, a new person, clean and fresh.

But it didn't last long. The following weekend, I was supposed to be going to Frank's home. I set out full of good intentions, but I got no further than the Dilly. Again I fell in with my junkie buddies. I didn't take heroin, but I took pills and got high.

I rang Frank. 'Listen,' I said. 'I'm in London. I'm high.'

Patient as ever, he arranged to drive into Soho and pick me up. He took me to his home. On the way he said: 'Audrey, it's become more urgent than ever to get you away from London. I think I know a place.'

That weekend he telephoned a family in Brighton and asked them to take me in. Within a few days, I was on the train and on my way.

The head of the family was a retired optician whom I called Pop. He lived with his daughter, Mary, and son-in-law, Ralph. They had three children, including a new baby, Timothy, whom I spent quite a lot of time looking after.

This was what I'd always dreamed of—living with a family. They were a good Christian family. Almost as soon as I arrived, they all knelt down to say prayers.

I thought, 'Crikey! Frank's moved me in with a crowd of Holy Joes!' But I had come here to start a new life, so I knelt down with them.

It was a very loving family situation, but, quite honestly, it scared me stiff. The longer I stayed, the harder I found it to cope. They were deeply religious, and I found myself foundering out of my depth. When they went to church I went with them, but it was purely for appearance. I wasn't taking anything in.

They had a mynah bird called Percy, and they were going to great trouble teaching it to speak. The family were coaxing it to say Christian phrases. But when they were out, I was teaching it to swear.

They had a piano. I hadn't played since the Farm Hill days. I was a bit rusty but I used to try playing tunes from the Old Redemption Hymnal. Whenever I went wrong, I'd swear—and the bird would pick it up!

I had a job as a petrol pump attendant. The months were passing by pleasantly enough, even though I found the family's religious lifestyle heavy going. But soon it was summer, and in the seaside sunshine I felt light-hearted and happy once more.

The summer, however, brought problems that Frank had not foreseen. He had arranged for me to go to Brighton to get away from the temptations of London.

But what happens at Brighton in the summer? Half of London decamps to be there—and that includes some of the junkie colony from the Dilly.

I first saw them when I was coming home from work, not my old friends but faces I half-recognised. They were hanging around that part of Brighton known as The Lanes. Junkies always seem to find a corner of every town and city, and even if I hadn't spotted faces I'd remembered from the past, I would still have known they were junkies. One junkie can recognise another a mile off, stoned or sober.

They were scruffy and pale, just like I had been before six months in bracing Brighton had put some colour in my cheeks. They had a sort of hang-dog look, aimless and pointless.

I felt excited. My heartbeat moved up a gear. No, I wasn't going to join them and ask them for a fix. Nothing stupid like that. I might talk to them and tell them how to get off drugs. I'd done it. So could they. But it was good to know that they were there, in case I needed them....

The following Saturday I went into town and drifted towards The Lanes. A group of us walked down to the beach. Some of them were cooking heroin before shooting it. When I saw that, I had to have some. Even after six clean months, the temptation was too great. I had plenty of money, and I bought a fix off one of the girls.

I didn't have too much, so I wasn't sick. But I never got home that night. A gang of us slept on the beach.

It was the middle of the morning when I got back and the family were at church. I was full of guilt and feeling terrible. I had come to them to be cured, and here I was full of dope again.

I didn't tell them, of course. I simply said I'd spent the night with a friend. But I found myself going to The Lanes more and more. It wasn't always heroin—more often it was pills. But I was dependent again. At least twice a week, I had to have my drugs.

I should have rung Frank Wilson. He could have helped me, and I trusted him. But I didn't. Instead, I tried to conceal my guilt—very difficult in the Christian family atmosphere—and this gave rise to conflicts and tensions. It got to the stage where I couldn't take it any more.

One night I had supper and went to bed along with the rest of the family. I lay in my bed pondering my dilemma. Pop and his family were so welcoming and kind. They had done their best to help me. But I had virtually spat in their faces with my weakness and disloyalty.

My bedroom was on the ground floor. I got out of bed without switching on the light and put on a pair of jeans and a sweater. Quietly I opened the window, and clambered over the sill to the lawn.

In the middle of the night I walked away from the house where I had been offered love and hospitality, and I never even went back to say thank you.

12

The Dance Goes On

How long I walked that night I do not know. Where I was making for I do not know. Just how far I got I do not know. And why I should leave my comfortable home in the middle of the night... I don't know that, either.

It was not the first time I had upped and run leaving behind all my clothes and the few possessions I had accumulated. It was totally irrational.

Looking back, I can offer an explanation—I think the only one. Satan, I believe, must have been in control of my mind, making me follow foolish impulses, setting me off on pointless quests, causing me to behave in a stupid way.

If I had been looking for drugs that night, I would have run in a different direction. I could easily have found the addicts I had befriended sleeping rough under Brighton Pier, and they would have shared their drugs with someone in need.

No, it wasn't drugs. It was something else. Satan was at the helm of my thinking processes. Far away from the coven, he was leading me a merry dance.

It's possible there was some witchcraft activity going on somewhere in Sussex that night, and I was being guided towards it. I had often heard voices in my head telling me of the coven meetings in Virginia Water, and even now witchcraft events cause a buzz in my head.

Thankfully, the police found me before I found any witches. A prowling patrol car spotted me and, because the officers were suspicious of a young woman stumbling along a dark road miles from anywhere, they picked me up and took me to their local station.

There I was given a cup of tea and a quizzing. Who was I? Where was I going? Where had I come from? Was I in trouble?

My trouble was much too big to share with a sergeant in a village police station. But I gave them my name and told them I had run away from my digs in Brighton. They telephoned Pop who confirmed I was who I said I was. But he refused to take me back. I don't blame him. He and his family had had enough of me.

Even though I hadn't taken drugs that day, I was in a state, crying and complaining that nobody wanted me. The police could see I was a junkie by the needle scars on my arms. They put me in a cell for the night. But I began to rant and rave and throw the furniture around.

They brought in a doctor to examine me. And because they were afraid I might harm myself, the doctor signed a care order committing me to a hospital for twenty-eight days for my own protection.

So the next morning I was taken to Severals Hospital in Colchester. It was a mental hospital and I was put into a secure ward where the doors were locked to stop the patients running away.

There was no doubt about it, I needed the treatment. I was depressed and disturbed, at times to the point of violence. I never hurt any of the staff or patients. I just did crazy things like tipping the beds over and ripping up the bedclothes.

Simple things triggered off these wild outbursts. Most of the time I was calm and well-behaved, helping the staff with the washing-up and other little jobs. Then something would happen and I would go berserk.

Sometimes it was while playing cards. There were about thirty people in that ward, and there would always be card schools on the go. I enjoyed playing rummy, but just getting a series of bad hands would be enough to throw me and make me lose my temper.

My deep and dark fits of depression were made worse because I couldn't explain to anybody what was at the bottom of them. I knew it was Satan getting his revenge. But I thought that if I told that to the psychiatrists, they would lock me up and I would be stuck in that hospital for life.

Strange, I didn't feel any desire for drugs—they might have made the depression easier to bear. I took the drugs the doctors prescribed for me. But I had no wish to get back on to the heroin treadmill.

Even though I felt ill, bored and unhappy, I had no wish to die. I still can't offer any explanation for my so-called suicide attempt while I was in that hospital.

It began one day while we were having lunch. I smuggled my knife into my pocket and the helpers never noticed it was missing when they cleared up the dishes. I went back to my room which I shared with another girl. For a while I lay on my bed. Then I took out the knife and tried to slash my wrists.

The knife was hardly sharp enough to cut through mashed potato. But I sawed away first at one wrist, then the other. It didn't go in very deeply but there was a lot of blood about and when my roommate came in she shrieked and raised the alarm.

The cuts were so shallow they didn't even need stitching. They were just bandaged up and I was paraded off to the doctors. They were more concerned with why I had done it than the minor injuries I had sustained.

But I couldn't tell them why. How could I tell them that Satan's favourite method of disposing with someone he has finished with is to prey on them until they kill themselves? How could I tell them a coven has the powers to kill by remote control and make it look either like an accident or suicide?

I cannot say if this was so in my case. I'm just not sure. But I do know I didn't want to die. Life was still precious, even though I was constantly depressed.

I think if Satan had really wanted me dead, he would have done a better job. He would have made sure the knife I used was sharper, or that my botched attempt had remained undiscovered so I would have lost more blood. Perhaps it was his way of telling me he was still in control and could finish me off whenever he liked, a sort of warning, giving me no peace as the warlock had said.

I put the bungled suicide down to Satan. It didn't occur to me at the time that God might have been protecting me. Now, looking back and seeing it in perspective, I realise that it was God who had saved me, as he was to save me from myself many more times in the future. And he too was in the business of giving no peace... until the time was right.

I had hardly given God a thought since Frank Wilson had taken me to that meeting at the Metropolitan Tabernacle. There had been a glow of hope that night when I left it. I had done nothing since to fan that glow, and encourage it to brighten into light. But I'm sure God, ever loving and merciful, was looking after me, as I had prayed that he would.

After the doctors had bandaged up my wrists, I was put into a padded cell. I was there for about twenty-four hours and I can tell you I didn't like it. There is nothing to do except sit and gaze and ponder. Even if you yell and scream, you can't be heard.

After this, the doctors decided my depression was severe enough to warrant ECT—electric shock treatment. They pass an electric current through the brain which lifts the black clouds of gloom, albeit temporarily.

I had to sign a form consenting to this treatment which I did. I thought it might make me forget those awful experiences in the coven. They were coming back regularly in terrifying nightmares that woke me up, screaming and sweating in terror. If the shock treatment would give me a peaceful night's sleep, I was eager to try it.

The effect was quite astonishing. I had about eight sessions. I'd wake up after each session not even knowing my name. For about an hour afterwards I didn't have a clue who I was or where I was. But the memory slowly returned—and so did the nightmares.

Night after night I relived the killing on the altar of that tiny baby. I could see the blood dripping from the baby's throat, and the warlock's expressionless face as he caught it in the chalice.

There were other nightmares. The matron at Dr Barnardo's appeared in some of them. I had called her the witch, and now in my dreams she came flying at me on a broomstick.

Even though it was summer, and there were gardens, I never went out during my time at Severals. We were not encouraged to go out. The hospital authorities regarded us as potential escapees. The summer went by and never once did I get out into the fresh air.

Nor did I have any visitors—not one person came to see me during the eight months I was there. My ward was a world on its own, with life just ticking by as if there was no outside world.

I began to get very resentful, and to ask myself the question: 'Whose fault is it that I am here? Who is to blame for the mess my life has become?'

The same answer kept recurring: my mother. It became an obsession that it was all my mother's fault. If she hadn't shunted me off to Dr Barnardo's, everything would have been all right. I decided how she must pay the price for ruining my life. I plotted to kill her.

To some people, it must seem laughable. Here I was, a former junkie, my powers to think rationally destroyed by heroin, lying on my bed in a mental hospital planning to murder my mother. But it was no idle fantasy. It was for real. I can only think my old dancing partner, Satan, must again have taken control of my thought processes.

I knew there was no chance of getting permission to leave the ward. So I plotted my escape, cunningly and secretly like those military prisoners you see in old war films.

First, I got hold of a knife—not to slash my wrists, but to scrape away at the plaster around the windowframe in my bedroom. The windows were too small for me to get through, so I had to remove the whole frame. It took about three nights before the frame was loose enough to move. Then I pulled the whole window into my room and, making sure I took the knife, I clambered out onto the drainpipe. My escape had begun.

I hadn't seen or heard from my mother since I was eleven years old. Now I was twenty-seven. What may have happened to her in those intervening years just didn't occur to me. She lived somewhere in Crewe, so that was where I should make for.

I began to climb down the pipe. Our ward was on the third floor, so it was quite a way down. Slowly, cautiously, gripping the pipe tightly, I lowered myself towards the garden. But I had forgotten one thing: the brackets holding the drainpipe to the wall.

My fingers, which were gripping the pipe as I slowly slid down, came into contact with the first bracket. Instead of holding the circular pipe, they splayed out causing me to lose my grip. My descent after that was considerably faster. How far I fell I'm not sure, but I landed on my feet.

It was not a happy landing. I smashed my right heel. The bone fractured into five pieces. Sonia, my roommate, was watching from the window. As soon as she realised my escape bid had gone wrong, she raised the alarm and staff came and took me back inside.

They strapped up the foot, which was becoming swollen and painful. That heel has given me trouble ever since and sometimes has been so painful I have had to wear a calliper to take the weight off it.

The doctors thought I had tried to throw myself out of the window to kill myself. Following the slashed wrists, it was a natural assumption. If they had known the truth—I was trying to escape so that I could murder my mother—they would have never let me out.

They gave me physiotherapy and electrical treatment to try to get my foot working again, but it would not heal. Apart from that, there was no other help at that hospital, no occupational therapy or anything that would help me get work when I left.

I was back in the old routine, and becoming very very bored. My behaviour had improved and there were few complaints about me, so they began to allow me to go out. I went on little shopping trips around Colchester.

It was on one of those trips that I decided not to go back. Instead I caught a train to London. I still had that vague plan in my mind to get revenge on my mother, and I still had my knife concealed inside the lower leg of my jeans.

There was a little bit of a kerfuffle when I arrived at Liverpool Street Station. I had a headache, so I bought a bottle of coke and some aspirins, and went to the ladies. But the attendant thought I was taking drugs, and called the law.

When they arrived, I told them that I had been a mental patient. They took me to St Thomas's Hospital in London where a psychiatrist saw me. He couldn't find anything wrong so I was handed over to a social worker. I told the social worker that I needed the train fare to go to Crewe to see my mother. I was given a ticket and £5 for a meal on the train.

As I boarded the train, I was still determined to murder my mother. The more I thought about her, the more I felt she was to blame for all my misfortunes. With her dead, I felt I would be released from whatever was causing me to have such a rotten life.

Satan, I am sure, put me on that train. And he was responsible for filling my heart with this obsessive hatred of my mother. I paced the corridor wondering how I was going to find her and kill her. But then Satan played another of his little tricks.

Through a window I spotted a young man sitting in a corner seat. There was something familiar about him. It wasn't his face that I recognised but his condition. This young man was a junkie, on a Cloud Nine high.

I started talking to him. He just grinned. He was stoned out of his mind. He put his hand in to his pocket and pulled out the workings—cigarette lighter, needle and a tiny pouch of heroin. It's strange about drug addicts. They will happily kill for a fix when they are desperate. But once on a high, they will give away every grain of heroin they possess to a fellow junkie.

I took the stuff to the toilet, cooked up the powder, and shot the heroin into my left arm. The buzz was immediate. It always is if you've been clean for a while, and I hadn't had anything for almost a year. Soon I was just as high as that young man and we sat grinning stupidly at each other as the train headed north.

I suppose Satan was chuckling. The sinister purpose for my journey had gone clean out of my mind. The first time the train stopped I got off. The station happened to be Birmingham, not Crewe. But it didn't matter to me where I was. I felt like a queen and I wondered why people were not bowing to me.

I was so enjoying my high as I wandered around the

railway station that I decided to go to the toilets. There I could sit in peace and enjoy it without anyone hassling me. Or so I thought. But it didn't last long. A zealous attendant called the police.

They saw immediately the state I was in and didn't even bother trying to find out who I was. They wheeled me straight into their car and dropped me at the drugs unit at All Saints' Hospital.

At first they couldn't get any sense out of me. I thought I was Queen Victoria, and kept insisting they should bow or curtsy. But it began to wear off, and the nagging depression slowly returned.

I stayed at All Saints' for several weeks and made friends there. One of the patients, Marilyn, became a particular friend. She was younger than me, about twenty. She had delightful looks, long blonde hair and a bubbly disposition to go with them.

Marilyn came from a good home. She had opted for a life of drugs because she felt rejected by her parents. We often discussed our different backgrounds. She felt that her parents were putting wealth and material things before her, and that was the cause of her dissatisfaction.

Marilyn offered me a joint—a cigarette stuffed with marijuana. We used to smoke marijuana, or cannabis as it is called nowadays, in the ward when there were no staff around. And I was soon to learn more potent drugs were available.

All Saints' Road is a long road, and in one of the little terraced houses a couple of minutes' walk from the hospital lived a young man who not only took drugs, but supplied them.

He had everything—heroin, pot, pills—and he let us have them cheaply. Some of the girls said the reason he could afford to was that he bought them cheaply from hard-up nurses at the hospital.

I bought a pile of pills from him that would have cost

£5 in London. All I gave him was a ten-bob note (50 pence). When I went back to the hospital as high as a kite, again I thought I was Queen Victoria.

I sat on my bed shouting: 'Bow to me, all of you. I am your Queen.'

Marilyn was in stitches. 'Shut up,' she said, 'or you'll give the game away and we'll all be in trouble.'

The only way they could keep me quiet was when Marilyn gently laid me down and said: 'Now, Your Majesty. It's time for your rest.' I went to sleep.

Marilyn had been admitted to the drugs unit as a heroin addict, and when they finished cleaning her up, she was discharged because her bed was needed. But she still continued to come to the hospital as a day patient so that the doctors could keep an eye on her and make sure she stayed clean. So I saw her nearly every day, and looked forward to our chats.

Even though she had been weaned off heroin, she still smoked pot, and we would share a joint when she came to see me. But one day she didn't turn up. I missed her but I didn't think very much about it.

I was more bothered when she didn't turn up the next day. It was a Saturday, and I wanted to ask her to go to the pictures with me. As well as friendship, there was a secondary motive. I was short of money and I knew she would treat me as she had in the past.

I hung around for about an hour wondering if she had been held up. But she didn't arrive at all. I wondered what had happened to her. Then I thought she had possibly gone away for the weekend. Strange, though, that she hadn't mentioned it.

By this stage of my treatment, I was free to come and go more or less as I pleased. I needed some pills, so I strolled down All Saints Road to the house where we always got them.

There was no reply when I knocked at the door. That

wasn't unusual. Often Dave, the fellow who ran the place, used to go away. But he hid the key in a place where those customers he trusted could find it. We used to help ourselves to whatever we needed, and pay later.

I opened the door. It was stuffy inside as if no doors or windows had been opened for a day or two. Then I saw the body. It was Marilyn, instantly recognisable by her long blonde hair.

She was lying on a blood-soaked divan with both of her wrists slashed open. She must have been lying undiscovered in that empty house for a couple of days.

My mouth opened, but I couldn't scream or cry. I just ran away. I wanted to get as far away from that dreadful sight as I could.

My mind was reeling. I thought of the time I had tried to cut my wrists. Now my friend had done the same thing—only in her case it had worked.

I should have reported it to the police, but I didn't. I just wanted to get away from her, as far away as possible.

My friend, my only friend, was dead. My footsteps rang as I pounded down All Saints Road. I swear I heard a mocking laugh echoing behind me as I blindly ran and ran.

13

Keeping the Door Shut

Breathless and tearful, I arrived at a crossroads. And it turned out to be a crossroads in my life. I had run as far as my legs would carry me. Now I needed a rest—and a drink.

Across the road was a building with cheerful music and lively sounds coming from it. Ah good! I thought. A pub where they are having a Saturday night knees-up. Just what I needed to cheer me up.

I was bursting for a large cool gin and tonic after the traumatic sight I had just seen. So in I went. But I couldn't see a bar. And no wonder—in my blind haste, I had run into Hockley Pentecostal Church.

I began to quake and feel sick. Satan didn't like me going into churches. He made sure that any such visit was as uncomfortable as possible. Sometimes in Brighton I had become so ill I'd blacked out in the middle of a service. On other occasions, I felt a powerful urge to stand up and scream obscenities at the preacher and congregation. Sometimes I actually had to walk out of churches because I was afraid that if I stayed I would do something terrible.

I had the same sort of feelings when I was with Christian people. I wanted to rave and rant at them, swear at them, shock them, for no reason other than that they were Christians. It seemed totally irrational, but in my heart I knew the reason. Satan didn't want me fraternising with the enemy.

I tried a variety of churches, but in none of them did I feel at ease. Once I tried to take communion wine, but I had to rush outside, violently sick. It reminded me of the time I had held a chalice to my lips and tasted the salty flavour of human blood.

When I accidentally rushed into that church at Hockley, it was a shock. I wanted to walk out, but my legs were aching after that run from the house where I had found my friend. I quietly sat and sobbed while I mourned Marilyn's death.

The service seemed to go on and on, but time meant nothing. After it had finished, I was aware of a little lady standing by me. She was talking to me, but I couldn't hear the words.

She spoke again. 'You need help, don't you dear?'

I collapsed and had to be helped to a seat. I told them I was a drug addict at All Saints. Two old ladies from the church, Miss Reeves and Miss Fisher, took me back to the hospital. Before they left me they said: 'We'll try to help you. We'll pray for you.'

They came to visit me a couple of days later. I discovered they were both ministers of the Pentecostal Church. They invited me to tea at their house. Miss Reeves said to me: 'Audrey, you'll kill yourself if you keep taking these drugs. Do you really want to give them up?'

I said, 'Yes. I really do. But it's so difficult.'

She said: 'We know just the place for you. There's a Christian Rehabilitation Farm at Redditch. We're sure they could help you.'

I decided to give it a try. It would be a nice change to live in the country after my spell in an inner-city mental institution. So I said: 'All right, then. I'll go.'

I had to be interviewed by the Director. Curiously, the

place was called Hill Farm, an inversion of the Dr Barnardo's Home which was Farm Hill. I passed my interview and moved in.

There were only two girls at Hill Farm. All the other residents were boys and men. One of the men, John Harper, was there to sort out his drink problem. Yes, Hill Farm was where I met my husband.

Church was compulsory every Sunday. But the prayers and hymns had no meaning for me. I used to get a loud buzzing in my head. It was like radio interference as if Satan was jamming the airwaves to make sure his dancing partner didn't get the message.

John, who was quiet and well-behaved, used to accompany me to church. I was a bad influence on him. We often disrupted the services by laughing and cracking jokes. It was a Jekyll-and-Hyde situation. Most of the time I was a charming Dr Jekyll, but once among the Christians I became a monstrous Hyde.

John worked away from the farm at a factory. I used to wait on the drive to walk up to the house with him when he got back in the evening. I moaned a lot about my job in the laundry, especially the ironing which I hated.

One day John said to me: 'You're always complaining. I don't know why we don't get married.'

Quick as a flash I said: 'Do you mean that?'

It was a strange sort of proposal. I had thought nobody would ever want to marry me, a scruffy junkie who had been a burglar and a streetgirl. I told John about my past, but he accepted me for what I was.

I told him most but not quite all. I didn't tell him, or anybody else, about my days as a witch, and my oath of allegiance to Satan. That was a secret I was not yet ready to disclose. I simply didn't feel strong enough.

Because of my unruly behaviour, I knew my days at Hill Farm were numbered. Once I lost my temper and smashed up my bedroom. The Director called me to his office. 'Leave now,' he thundered. 'I don't want you around another day.'

Leaving there made it more difficult to see John. But we decided we would get wed as soon as we could find somewhere to live. I got a job helping to look after a laundrette with a three-roomed flat above which we could have for nothing, so we set the date.

Even though we had no money, we had a lovely wedding at Rubery Parish Church. Mark, the vicar of Rubery where I had been lodging, married us—for nothing. The choir sang for us—for nothing. The Women's Institute did the reception—for nothing. We even had champagne.

I needed somebody to give me away, and I got in touch with Pop in Brighton. After the merry dance I had led him and his family when I stayed with them, I was surprised that he agreed. He was as good as gold.

The early days of a marriage are a happy time for most people, and they were for me. There was no interference from Satan. I was enjoying a lovely lull. I often asked myself: 'Has he given up on me? Is he going to leave me alone now?' I should have known it couldn't last.

In Birmingham one morning I bumped into a girl I'd known at All Saints. She gave me a handful of purple hearts for old times' sake. Foolishly I accepted them. They are not addictive, but having done for so long without the psychological prop of soft drugs, here I was depending on it again.

For a few days I took them sneakily. John didn't realise I was up to my old tricks. Then I thought: 'This can't go on. I'll be back in the gutter. Only this time John will be with me.'

I went to my doctor and told him about my murky past with drugs. When I convinced him I wanted to give them up, he arranged for me to become a voluntary patient at Barnsley Hall, a hospital at Bromsgrove. It was smaller and more intimate than the big hospitals I was used to. We were encouraged to do things to occupy us, so I started drawing and painting again.

One of the doctors saw my efforts and was horrified. 'What's the matter with you?' he asked. 'You keep drawing death pictures.'

I looked at the sheets of paper. He was right. Every one had drawings of death. There were hangman's nooses, guns, guillotines, people burning to death on bonfires. It seemed I was obsessed with death, and every time I sat down to draw or paint, some unseen force seemed to guide my hand to produce these morbid pictures.

Could it be Satan still lurking in the background? Had the coven put a curse of death on me? I began to worry about my safety, and that led to a bout of deep depression.

When I returned home after three weeks, my moods made me impossible to live with. But John has always been a patient, understanding man, and even though I couldn't tell him what was at the root of my troubles, he pampered and petted me and brought me through it.

About this time we began to try for a baby. The thought occurred to me that a baby might be my salvation. And we didn't have long to wait before the signs came that we had succeeded. Alas, my soaring hopes were soon dashed to the ground. Before two months were up, I had miscarried. Three times in all I had miscarriages, and I began to think I would never have a child.

There were more ominous thoughts accompanying this miserable feeling of failure. Was it God punishing me for my wicked past? Or, more likely, was it Satan trying to make sure I would never know peace of mind?

I remember sitting in the flat one day reading the Bible. A friend had given it to me, suggesting that if I read the Psalms they might give me some comfort. They are so beautifully written, and so inspiring.

But suddenly I wanted to destroy these beautiful words. I don't know why I did it, but I went through that Bible ripping out every page and screwing it up. The room was knee-deep in paper when I had finished, but I felt a sort of inner glow that I had defiled God's teachings.

The longing for my own baby kept returning. I knew there was nothing wrong with my child-bearing mechanism. After all, I had given birth to two perfectly healthy babies—little Robin, whom I gave away, and the warlock's child which I never saw.

After the third miscarriage, the doctors said I would never be able to have a baby. But they were wrong. In spite of their verdict, I did conceive again.

As the birth date got nearer, a terrible fear gripped me. Suppose Satan lets me have the baby—but it's deformed? That would be a typical trick after all he had put me through. It was a torment that stayed with me from the moment I discovered I was pregnant until the birth—a black nightmare that was with me asleep and awake.

The specialist I was seeing had put me on an anti-abortion drug to prevent my body rejecting the tiny being growing inside me. But I wondered if this drug was a match for Satan's powers.

After all the troubles and traumas, the delivery was simple and uncomplicated. It was like a dream. And there I was, looking at my baby daughter, the child I thought I would never have.

We decided to call her Elizabeth, but she soon became Liz. She was born at three a.m. on February 9, 1973. I couldn't believe it had actually happened, even when she was snuggling against me crying to be fed. I held her and whispered a little prayer: 'Thank you, God. You were there all the time. Thank you for looking after me and giving me this beautiful baby.'

But if I thought Satan would now give up and go away, I was wrong. The devil does not relinquish his dancing partners so easily. It wasn't long before he showed his hand again.

One night, when she was just a few months old, Liz just wouldn't stop crying. It went on and on, getting louder and louder. I stood by her cot, and I felt a quivering wave of evil pass through me. It seemed to start in my head and move like a tingling sensation right through my body to my fingers and toes. I looked down at my pretty little daughter debating whether to put the pillow over her face and smother her.

It wasn't simply a fit of temper. It was a murderous compulsion that I managed somehow to control. I'm sure other mothers have them, but to me it seemed as if Satan was at work, trying to get me to kill my child.

I couldn't even share my fears with the health visitor— she'd think I was insane. I became over-protective of Liz, frightened even to smack her. A bruise on her arm, any tiny mark, and they might start checking on my background. I thought they would be sure to take her away from me.

So I loved Liz deeply and obsessively. But I kept getting these feelings that there was a power which wanted to harm her, using me as the instrument. When she was about twelve months old, I had another of these strange urges. I had had a sleepless night with her crying, and all through the morning she continued. Nothing would stop her, and it got to the stage where I couldn't take any more. So I held her up to my shoulder and I felt an impulse to squeeze her face against me to shut her up so that she couldn't breathe.

I held her tightly for a second or two before realising what I was doing. I was aghast. Was Satan trying to make me murder my own child? Was this how the curse would work—destroying me by impelling me to destroy my baby?

Horrified with myself, I just threw her into her crib and walked out of the room, slamming the door to create a physical, protective barrier between us.

To try to regain my self-control, I went downstairs, and there I met a neighbour, who was a nurse. I hid my shame from her, and said: 'Liz is playing up.'

The neighbour, Betty, said: 'Shall I have a look at her?' She came up to the flat, picked Liz up and said: 'She's just a bit upset.'

But she must have seen something in my face that told her I was near the end of my tether. She said: 'Shall I have her for a few hours to give you a break?'

'I'd be glad if you would,' I said. I welcomed her offer. Not just for my sake, but for Liz's as well.

I hadn't had a single nightmare since Liz had been born. But I had one that night—the worst ever. I dreamt of the coven and my initiation ceremony. But when the warlock came to cut the baby's throat, I looked at the tiny girl's face. It was Liz.

That nightmare took a lot of getting over. For weeks I had shivering fits whenever I thought about it. It caused me to pamper my baby all the more, and as she grew older and responded, I became more loving and protective. No way was Satan going to get her, I'd see to that!

Liz dominated our lives. I would be with her all day, and when John came home in the evening from his job at a glassware factory, he took over. It left little time for anything else, even going to church.

My churchgoing suffered for two or three years after Liz's birth. I hardly went at all. Perhaps that's why, during this time, I wasn't having a lot of bother with Satan. It was when I went to church regularly and involved myself in prayer and church activities that the conflicts arose.

I didn't want Liz to be christened. I suppose I felt it would lead to trouble. Once or twice if we were with friends and they suggested going to church, we might accompany them and take Liz, but these visits were rare.

She was well behaved in church, and never caused us any bother or embarrassment. It was Mum who was the trouble. If I wasn't squabbling with my fellow worshippers, I would become disturbed and start arguing with John when we got home. It always led to aggravation instead of the peace of mind worship should bring.

Frankly, at this time, I was afraid of going to church. Our lives were sweet and calm and I didn't want to rock the boat. My life seemed to be ruled by fear—fear that something would happen to spoil our happiness. And, more important, fear that something might happen to Liz.

I noticed something in my own mind that disturbed me. If I was reading a newspaper and I saw an advert for a psychic fair, I would get excited, and feel slightly drawn to it. Or if I read that a medium was giving a demonstration, I'd feel that I was missing out by not going.

These occult events could stir me and give me a buzz. I felt it was a sign that if the coven really wanted me back, they had only to send one of their telepathic messages and I would go running to them.

I hate to say it, but God was shut out of our lives during this period. We were warm and cosy in our flat, and I felt that if we opened the door to admit God, we'd be letting Satan in as well.

It's a terrible thing for a so-called Christian (as I now thought of myself) to say, but I felt the only way to exclude Satan from my life was by keeping the door firmly shut against God.

14

Found Out

On the surface our lives seemed quite ordinary.But beneath this veneer of suburban normality, a cauldron of emotions was bubbling away. It was like a timebomb. I knew that sometime it would explode, but I had no idea just when.

The days were not too bad. But the nights were hellish. Vivid nightmares flickered through my sleep, reminding me of my past, casting sinister shadows over my future. They left me tired and drained of energy every morning.

We had moved from our flat over the laundrette at Rubery to a three-bedroomed house at Droitwich. Our new home had a garden and was on a nice modern estate with pleasant shops and friendly neighbours.

They knew nothing about my past, of course. I'm sure some of the neighbours in their neat houses would have been horrified if they knew that a former witch, albeit a reformed one, had moved into their midst—especially if they had an inkling of the terrible things I had seen and done.

John was earning good money working as a postman, and I got a job as a school dinner lady to bring in a few extra pounds. We would have been happy and settled if it wasn't for those desperate nightmares when my past came back to haunt me.

Even though I tried to be a good Christian, my faith was not strong at this time. I was wavering. I began to think, 'Oh God. You're not looking after me again.' It was a repeat of those days of doubt and self-pity when I was in the mental hospital.

We started going to the local Pentecostal church—a lovely little church at the top of a hill, and after a few visits we took Liz, when she was four, for her dedication. We were doing all the right things as Christians, but it wasn't working out.

At that time I didn't immediately connect it with the curse that had been put upon me. But it wasn't long before I came to realise that having made a contract with the devil, he wasn't going to allow me to back out.

We only went to the church four times after Liz's dedication. We had felt that we ought to try it but somehow it didn't do anything for me. I had never really got over those dreadful feelings of nausea every time I entered a church.

I remember having an awful guilt complex about not going, and walking miles all round the estate so that I wouldn't have to pass the pastor's house and risk meeting him.

But when I looked at those other people in the congregation they appeared so lovely and squeaky clean, and I didn't feel like that because of my past. I used to scrub myself in the bath until my skin was red and raw but it made no difference. I still felt dirty—contaminated by evil.

I wasn't taking drugs, or doing anything else wrong. But my past was haunting me. I kept thinking how inadequate I was compared with the other churchgoers, and asking myself how I could ever come up to their standards.

Now I've got to know some of those people. I've told them of my feelings and we've had a jolly good laugh about it. But at the time I wasn't laughing. They gave the impression of being pure and holy—and I felt I was tainted and sinful.

Not only did we stop going to church, I didn't mind not going. Somehow the conviction that the church would help me had fizzled away. Things were good—and, feeling I didn't need my faith, I pushed it into second place. We were pottering along quite happily. I had stopped my daily Bible readings. My relationship with God was non-existent.

I didn't know until later that even though we had stopped going to church, members of the congregation were regularly saying prayers for us pleading that we would return. I heard about this later when I bumped into the pastor. They were very keen for us all to start attending church again. The pastor even came around to the house and said that, as committed Christians, we should.

I don't know why, but somehow I hadn't got the urge. Even when the pastor died, I didn't go to his funeral. I just didn't think anything of it.

Then things started going wrong. John had moved from the Post Office to a better paid job at a factory making pipes. The extra money was great. But his health packed up, and he had to give up working and stay at home with high blood pressure.

Suddenly the sunshine had gone out of our lives, and a great depressing shadow took its place. There was no money. Then my health, too, began to suffer. John wouldn't go outside the house, in case people should see he wasn't working. It had a terrible effect on him—and it rubbed off on me.

I've always had a short fuse, and lose my temper quickly, but it's much worse when things are going badly. Now things were going very badly, and I must have been unbearable. I'm surprised John stayed with me.

I remember having an argument with Liz. I grabbed

her arm and tugged it. I heard a click. I thought I'd broken her arm. I was so distraught I rang the Samaritans, and a lady came round and helped me to cool down. She took Liz for a walk to get her out of my hair until I recovered.

My feelings, when I look back on them, were totally irrational. I felt that the only way I could be a Christian was to get away from Liz and John for a while. And I thought they would have a better chance of finding happiness without me. Really it was nonsense. We are a very strongly bonded family, and we needed to stay together then with our troubles more than at any time. But that was the peculiar way I was thinking.

At times I got so angry it frightened me. I didn't attack John, or throw things around, but I used to have terrible tantrums. I was afraid I would do something desperate, especially to Liz. More than once I locked her in her bedroom and walked away, fearful that if she came close to me I might strike her, or hurt her in some way.

It was John who led us back to the church. One night he was feeling so utterly depressed with his own inability to work and my black moods he decided to go to a prayer meeting at the little church at the top of the hill we had neglected for so long.

The change in him when he came back was amazing. He seemed to be floating on air. He had a silly grin on his face and he was happy and joking—yet, when he had left the house a couple of hours earlier, he seemed to have the weight of the world on his shoulders.

Then Liz decided she wanted to go to the church with her dad. She was eight now and had started going to a young people's group at another church, but it wasn't very lively and the Pentecostal service had more fun and music.

They went several times together, leaving me at home. But then I relented—I decided I wanted to go with them.

It wasn't so much for the service as for the company of my family. I didn't want to be left out.

That was the start of an amazing period of our lives. There was a retired minister preaching that night, a man called Tom Jones. We got to know Pastor Tom and his wife. They were wonderful people, one of the finest couples I have ever met. They had no children of their own, but they were beautiful with children. Liz had no grandparents of her own, but that's what Tom and his wife became to her.

The depression lifted, and the sun came out again. My black moods vanished. In fact, people from the church who saw our happiness began bringing their troubles to us. I became an unofficial counsellor on a variety of problems—marital, spiritual, bringing up children, all sorts of topics. It was lovely helping people with their problems, rather than focusing on mine all the time.

God, and the church, had become a part of my life again, the most important part. I had found my faith again. It was the start of an idyllic six months, the most peaceful period of my life.

Our home was always full of people who came to talk over their troubles. When they went away, it was not always with the problem solved, but they felt spiritually uplifted because they had had such a happy time with us. I was sure they wouldn't have been so keen to accept my advice if they had known about my own sordid past.

The church had assumed once more its rightful position in my life, and I really felt in tune with God. At last I believed that God had forgiven my wicked past. I still had the occasional nightmare, but only rarely.

Tom and Margaret were frequent visitors to our house. I used to talk to them about all sorts of things, but I could never bring myself to share my past with Tom. He knew, however, that I had problems. He was a perceptive man, and very godly, and I suppose such people have a way of discerning when someone has been contaminated by the devil.

But then Tom had a stroke and died. I went to his funeral, and afterwards, when I went home, I discovered something that frightened me. I still had some of the powers I had cultivated in the coven. I was able to call up Tom—at least it seemed to be Tom—after he had departed, and he came to the house and had a conversation with me.

I now realise this was a deception. The dead, I came to learn later, do not return. But at the time Satan was still occupying my mind, and I believed Tom had come back to talk to me.

John heard my voice from the bedroom. 'Who are you talking to?' he called.

'Tom,' I replied.

'Don't be silly. He's dead. We buried him this morning.'

'Yes, but he still came to see me.'

We had a long conversation, Tom and I. I told him all about my present problems, and some of the things from my past. I poured my heart out to him. I wished afterwards I'd told him some of these things while he was alive.

With Tom's death, the light once again went out of my life. Evil thoughts returned, and dark depressing moods. I could feel something stirring within me. Satan had persuaded me that he had brought back Tom and presented him to me. His influence was growing again.

There was a new pastor at the church, youthful and pleasant. But I didn't want to go back there. All I wanted, at this dreadful stage, was to see the church burnt down. I tried a couple of times to go back. But I found myself looking at the faces of my friends, and laughing at them.

The new pastor, Jim Burton, was furious, and quite rightly. 'God will not be mocked!' he thundered at me.

Before he died, Tom told Jim that he guessed I had a deep, dark problem in my past. Tom was still able to walk about at this stage. One night the pair of them came to my house. I hadn't invited them, but they came in and began to pray.

Jim was calling: 'In the name of Jesus, get out!' They were trying to exorcise Satan from my home and from my life. But it didn't work. I was resisting and I began to mock them. I finished up telling them to go away.

My feelings towards the pastor and the congregation were murderous. I didn't just want to see the church burnt down—I wanted to strike the match, preferably with all of them inside.

My mind was in such a turmoil that I actually sat down and plotted to do this dreadful deed, much as I had plotted to kill my mother years before. Once again, however, I didn't put it into practice. Yet something had to happen with the pressures and hatreds that were building up in my mind, and fast reaching detonation point.

Something did happen. I didn't destroy the church and congregation. I tried to destroy myself instead. I took an overdose.

John found me in bed, realised something was wrong and called the doctor. I came to in the casualty ward of Worcester Infirmary. They had pumped out my stomach and put me in a bed.

I don't know how many sleeping pills I had taken. But when I woke up, amazingly I didn't feel too bad. The nurses were not very sympathetic. I can't really blame them. I don't think they liked their time being wasted by OD patients.

I came home. They may have pumped out my stomach, but the poison was still in my mind. Christmas was approaching, and Liz was getting excited but I just didn't want to know. Most of the time I was padding around the house like a zombie, and the only time I came to life was to have a row and be nasty to my family.

It's hard to describe how I felt. It was as if someone had come along and wiped out all the joy and beauty in my life, leaving behind parts that were dirty and ugly.

It had to happen again, and it did. Within days I took a second overdose. There were plenty of drugs in my cupboard—sleeping tablets, pethadine, valium, stuff that had been prescribed for me in the past when I was suffering pain with my ankle. What I took I do not know, but it must have been a pretty lethal concoction.

Again I was rushed to hospital and put on the stomach pump. But this time, when they flushed the drugs out of me, I was admitted to the psychiatric unit.

I remember hobbling into the ward with a walking stick, because my ankle was giving me trouble. And I had the shock of my life. There, sitting on the bed the nurse was preparing for me, was a miniature hooded figure. Surely this was the fellow at the bottom of all my troubles.

I was sure it was Satan manifesting himself to me. He was propped up on the pillow, grinning. It was almost as if he was gloating over me: 'Here you are, my girl. You should know better than to try to get away from me. We made a deal and you've got to stick to it.'

The other people who were there couldn't see anyone, that much I could tell. But to me he was very real, and very dangerous. I flew at him and began to swing at him with my walking stick.

To the nurses and doctors, it must have been a strange sight, seeing a woman whacking at a pillow and screaming: 'Get away. Get away.' But I suppose, in psychiatric wards, they are used to strange goings-on.

They said I was barmy, and what I had seen was a hallucination after using drugs. But at that time I wasn't using drugs. I knew I had had a visit from Satan. He had come to remind me of the curse, and the words of the warlock when he had visited me all those years ago.

What had he said? 'Wherever you go, whatever you do, you will never, never have peace of mind. You have deserted us—and Satan will pursue you.'

Well, here he was! He had come to remind me in person. He had a face very similar to the warlock, pale, gaunt, with deep black empty eyes, and a black hood masking part of it. He was small, the size of a doll, and he just sat on the pillow with his knees drawn up. But I was terrified—mostly by that mocking grin.

He vanished after I attacked him with my stick. But for days I felt he was still lurking around, and would come back. Every night one of the nurses would bring a torch and search all round the room and under the bed to make sure there was nothing there before I could get to sleep.

I am sure most of the staff thought I was a nut case. But there was one young man who realised what was happening to me. He was a Christian, and he was working on my ward.

He came up to me the morning after my little tussle with that unwelcome visitor and quietly said: 'You know, God does know you're here.'

'No he doesn't,' I replied. 'He's turned his back on me.' I was convinced by now that God had given me up as a bad job.

They kept me in that hospital for two weeks. As he was discharging me the doctor said, 'You've got to learn to live with yourself. The answer can't come out of a bottle of pills.'

He was right. That's exactly what was wrong with me—I couldn't live with myself. Yet, if God was what people said he was, I should be able to. I had asked him to help me. I had asked him to give me a new life. But I was desperate, because I hadn't got that new life.

I returned home just a couple of days before Christmas. Liz had been looking forward to it, but for me it had no meaning. Somehow I rallied round and served up a Christmas dinner, but there was no spirit, no joy. I think of it now as the Christmas I missed.

I was drifting through the days and weeks with no enthusiasm, no purpose. We had stopped going to church. It seemed to have no attraction, and I don't think it would have given me any comfort had I gone.

But then I remembered a promise I had made to Tom before he died. Though I had never told him I had been a witch, I felt he knew. He had taken me by the hand when he was close to death and said: 'Promise me you'll keep searching. Don't give up.'

I had promised, just to humour him. But now it came back to me. And something else came back to me—a meeting with a young minister, Roy Davies. We had met at Tom's funeral, and he had put his arm around me and said: 'Why don't you come and see us some time?'

For weeks and months I had done nothing. But remembering the promise gave me a glimmer of fresh hope. And I also remembered the invitation from Roy who was the minister at Emmanuel Pentecostal Church in Stourport, ten miles from where we lived.

We started going over on Sundays. At first, I didn't particularly enjoy the meetings. I didn't believe God could do anything for me. But I wanted to participate.

I was still getting evil thoughts, even while in church. I wanted to stand on a seat and shout, 'To hell with the lot of you!' or throw communion wine over everybody. I was never sure that I would be able to restrain myself. As an insurance, I usually took a valium tablet before meetings to help me control myself.

Sometimes we went to church twice on a Sunday, driving over for the morning service and taking sandwiches for a picnic lunch before the evening service. It sounds as if we were enthusiastic churchgoers, but I wasn't. I just kept going grudgingly because of my promise to Tom that I would keep on searching.

One night, after the meeting, I was standing by the car talking to John. We were just about to drive home. Then, suddenly, something came over me. What caused it I don't know, but I exclaimed, 'If I don't get help now, I'll never survive.'

I ran back into the church, and I said to Roy: 'You've got to help me. I'm dying!'

He studied me for a moment. Then he said: 'Yes, I know.'

The first time I was admitted to hospital, after my years of drug-taking and sordid living, I wanted to die. There was a difference now. I felt I was dying from the pressures of the curse—but I wanted to live.

Roy said: 'I am going to ask God what is wrong, and what I need to do to put it right.'

He knelt down, and he began to pray. Then he stood up, looked at me very gently, and said: 'You've been involved in witchcraft, haven't you Audrey?'

My mouth gaped open. How could he know? This was my secret—I had told nobody, not even Tom, although he had guessed there was something black and sinister in my past. I recognised that the information could have come from only one source—from God, while Roy was praying.

I was ashamed. I wanted the floor to open and swallow me up. I half expected him to back away. But he persisted: 'How long ago was it?'

'A very long time ago,' I mumbled.

I started crying. For me to cry was rare. I'd had a pretty hard upbringing without much time for tears. But now I was sobbing uncontrollably. Then I realised Roy was crying with me. He put his arm around me and said: 'Now we know, we love you all the more.'

Roy never told anybody else about my past. I love him

for that. What he said was that he would come over to my house, the very next night, and talk about it.

When he came, I told him everything. I gave him a full description of the initiation ceremony that unforgettable night at the coven. I told him about drinking the blood—and the poor little baby who was sacrificed to supply it.

He sat there listening quietly as the horrific details unfolded. I kept nothing back. He was so compassionate. At last, I felt, I had found someone who could help me win my struggle.

He asked about the curse, and how it had affected my life. I looked back over all the dreadful things that had happened to me, warping my mind and dictating my evil deeds. I recalled the nightmares which came to torment me. I remembered the words of the warlock: 'You shall have no peace.'

I told Roy about these things saying, 'The curse has been very effective. It's ruined my life.'

'God can break that,' Roy said quietly.

I wasn't sure. 'How?' I asked. 'I'm already a Christian—but I'm still burdened with it.'

Roy explained to me that you can be a Christian and still be under Satan's influence. I wasn't completely confident, but I was prepared to try anything. 'What do I have to do?'

We arranged that I would go to the church to meet him on an evening three days after he called at my house. Those three days were an agony. I gave my family hell. A lot of the time I felt suicidal. And the nights were even worse.

The nightmares I experienced those three nights were more frightening than I had ever had with all sorts of nameless terrors crowding in on me. It was Satan having his last fling—if I could only believe it really was his last.

When I went to the church to keep my rendezvous, I had murder in my heart. I didn't remember putting them there, but in one of the pockets of my coat was a box of pills, and in the other was a pair of long-bladed scissors.

15

'The Back Door's Shut'

Just what happened during the three hours of my exorcism I do not know. It remains a blank in my mind. I can remember going to the church that night, reluctantly I might add. I knew Roy was going to try to help me, but I didn't place much hope on his chances.

I remember going—and I remember coming away with a glorious feeling of relief that, at last, I was free of Satan. But I have no recollection of what happened in between, and know only the skimpy details I've been told since.

Those three hours must be the most important of my life, and certainly the most important of my story. I'm quite sure I would not be alive to tell it if that curse had stayed with me—if Roy Davies and his colleagues and the power of God's grace in their prayers had not successfully delivered me from evil.

So I have asked Roy, whose home is at Glyn Neath in South Wales, to fill in this blank by recounting what happened during those vital three hours. This chapter of my book belongs to him. So I'll let him tell it....

*   *   *

I first met Audrey, as she says, at Tom Jones' funeral. At that very first meeting I could see something was troubling her, something deep-rooted. But I had no idea what it was.

I got my first inkling when she started coming to church. When I offered her the chalice of communion wine, there was a hesitancy. She would take it, but with great reluctance, and her face would afterwards become contorted as if she had taken something distasteful.

When I heard her explanation, I was not surprised. Communion wine represents the blood of Christ. But to Audrey it brought back fearful memories of when she had seen that little child sacrificed and been forced to drink its blood.

I have had previous experiences with people who have been involved with occult practices and mysticism. I have exorcised homes where I have seen furniture move round, pictures fall off walls, even a sack of potatoes move from one side of a room to the other with nobody touching it.

There are many people who refuse to believe such things occur. I can understand their scepticism. But true Christians know about God's powers, and they are all too aware that Satan has powers as well.

Until I met Audrey, I had never had to deal with a case in which the demon spirits were so well established. They had occupied her soul for close on quarter of a century. But I was confident I could release her from that curse. Not by myself, of course, but with God's help.

Even before she had confided in me, I knew it was witchcraft that was the cause of her problems. There was nothing magical about my diagnosis. God had told me while I was praying for her.

There are some people who cannot, or will not, accept

that demon spirits can occupy a mind. They think that every person whose behaviour is erratic or irrational or downright evil must be mentally deranged.

They are wrong. I have come across many people who are, to a greater or lesser degree, insane. I can tell the difference between insanity and evil spirits.

Audrey's problem could never have been cured by valium or psychoanalysis or lobotomy. It was spiritual. But the spirits had been there a long time. They obviously felt they had a right of tenancy. They would take some kicking out.

It made me very sad that her life had been ruined by Satan's deception. It also made me angry. I suppose you could call it righteous indignation, but I was annoyed at what the people in the coven and Satan's evil force had done to her.

I think Audrey's basic problem sprang from a lack of love in her early life. She often said to me, 'There was nobody to love me, and nobody for me to love back. I don't know how to love.'

Those feelings of rejection and the lack of a family background to fall back on, so very important when you are emotionally disturbed, made her a sitting target for Satan, and for his followers in that coven.

Audrey was to come to Emmanuel Pentecostal Church in Stourport where I was minister. I had arranged for another minister, Bill O'Leary, an Irish friend of mine who has a church in Kidderminster, and one of the elders from my church, Brian Turner, to be with me that night. I realised that delivering Audrey from such deep-rooted problems would be difficult and take time, and that I would need help.

There was no plan of campaign worked out in advance. It would be done simply by prayer. I would call upon God to banish the demons from her, and we would pray together until she was released from the curse.

Bill and Brian were there, but no Audrey. I found her waiting nervously outside the church. She was reluctant about coming inside. You could almost see the inner turmoil: 'I want to be free but I don't want to go in there.'

I took her by the hand and gently led her inside the church, and we sat down in a circle so that we could all see each other. The exorcism, or the deliverance ministry as I'd prefer to call it, began.

The first thing I had to do was to identify the areas in her life where she had sinned, such as recruiting children for pornography, or stealing, and get her to admit that it was wrong.

We would pray quietly and calmly for a while, then I would say to Audrey: 'I'm not speaking to you now. I'm speaking to the spirit.'

These spirits are not Mickey Mouse things. They are real and dangerous. When we identified the various spirits which were controlling her activities, each one had to be challenged and banished.

In a much more strident voice than when we were praying, I uttered the challenge: 'I command you in the name of Jesus Christ to be subject to me as a child of God. I command you to leave this body now.'

Sometimes the spirit left immediately and we could move on to deal with the next one. Other times the spirit felt it had a right of residency, having been in occupation a long time. These spirits were more difficult to shift. With some of them we really had to struggle.

There were spirits of self-destruction, jealousy, suicide, murder, and various other sinful activities that caused a great deal of upset in Audrey whenever they were challenged.

The spirits would reply to the challenge through Audrey. It was her speech mechanism that they used, but her voice would change according to which spirit was defying the challenge.

Sometimes her voice would be calm and gentle. Other times it would be harsh. On some occasions it was high pitched. On others it was a deep throaty growl. And her face altered to go with these different voices. Sometimes it was contorted as if she was suffering pain.

The stress was so intense that several times during the deliverance she had choking fits and began to cough up sputum. I had expected this, and we had a towel ready to wipe her mouth.

I was told by God that she had something dangerous in the pockets of her coat.

'What have you got in your pockets?' I asked her.

'Nothing,' she replied.

'Oh yes, you have. Come on Audrey. Whatever it is, give it to me.'

'I haven't got anything,' she insisted.

Then I thundered at her: 'In the name of the Lord, I command you to give me whatever you have in those pockets.'

Meekly, she obeyed. Her right hand came out holding a long-bladed pair of scissors. In the left hand she was holding a box of pills.

'What are they for?' I asked her.

Holding up the scissors, she said: 'These are to stab you with.'

Then she held out the pills. 'And these are for me to take after I've killed you.'

But by this stage the spirit of aggression had been banished from her and she handed over the pills and scissors without any fuss. I was thankful God had revealed the scissors then and not earlier!

Before I had challenged the various spirits, I had to get Audrey to renounce the sinful activity that it had controlled, to repent of it and to ask God's forgiveness.

We were not prepared for the reaction when we moved to the area of witchcraft. I gave her a slip of paper on which I had written a form of renunciation, and I asked her to read the words aloud.

I asked her to renounce witchcraft, and to repent for having been a witch. Both of these she did, although I had a feeling that the spirits were making her lie. That is one of the difficulties—the lying of Satan.

The Bible tells us about Satan's lying. To him, a lie is as good as the truth, better than the truth. Sometimes, with Audrey's responses, we could not be sure if it was her truthful reply—or the spirit trying to fob us off with a lie.

So I went through the responses about witchcraft again. All went well until I asked her to confess that Jesus Christ is the Lord.

She said: 'Jesus Christ is the Lord.'

Then I said, 'Confess Jesus Christ is my Lord.

She said: 'Yes, I confess Jesus Christ is my Lord.'

Then I told her to repeat: 'Jesus Christ is Lord over witchcraft.'

There was an explosion. 'He is not Lord over witchcraft. Satan is Lord over witchcraft.'

With that she lunged forward with her hands aimed towards Bill's throat. But something stopped her as though an invisible barrier had suddenly been raised between them. She stopped as if she had crashed into a wall.

That was the only time she made a physical protest, but several times she swore and shouted and uttered profanities. The voice she used was not her own. It was the last defiant protests of the departing spirits.

There were tears of anger and sorrow. More than once she threatened to leave, but I commanded her to stay, using the Lord's name. Once she got up from her seat and made to walk towards the door. But before she had taken more than two steps, she fell to the floor. It was as if she had been pole-axed. We had to pick her up and seat her. It was some moments before she recovered.

That, I believe, was an act of God. He believed that what we were doing was right, and was determined that Audrey should stay and see it through.

At the end of the three-hour marathon we felt drained, and I know Audrey did as well. It was not a picnic, but a battle which we had to win.

There was a feeling of relief when Audrey was able to make her final confession with real joy—that Jesus Christ was Lord, and his blood had cleansed every area we had spoken about... murder, theft, witchcraft, pornography... and that Jesus Christ was the rightful Lord of all those areas.

One of the important spirits we dealt with that night was the spirit of hate. Up to this time, Audrey had only known hatred, rarely experienced love—either giving it, or receiving it.

But we delivered that spirit from her. And people who knew her before and after have noticed the difference. Now she can love and she can teach others to love.

Audrey's problem was that she was locked into her dreadful past. She was trapped by her own history and couldn't move forward. But we are children of destiny. Now she is equipped to fulfil that destiny.

She is fulfilling part of that destiny by telling her story. People in the church are all too aware of the growth of witchcraft in this country.

Let the dreadful things that Audrey has witnessed be a warning to others. She is in my prayers, and I pray that her warning will be heeded.

*   *   *

When Roy told me later about the scissors and the pills, I was horrified. Here was a man I had grown to love, while deep within my tortured mind a plot was hatching to murder him, and then kill myself.

But this was Satan's last stand. When he knows he is about to be defeated, he usually tries something desperate. This was his final devilish act before relinquishing his dancing partner.

It's hard to put down my feelings when I left the church that night. I knew Satan no longer controlled me. I felt lightheaded, as though I'd been drinking alcohol without getting drunk. Somehow my body felt lighter and clean—as if someone had taken a lump off my back and rinsed me out with washing-up liquid.

There was relief, there was joy, and for the first time for years, I didn't have that feeling that I was contaminated with sin. But most of all there was a glowing reassurance inside me that everything was going to be all right in my life from now on—my relationships with John, with Liz, with myself, and my relationship with God.

All of these relationships had been threatened by the way I behaved under the influence of the curse. But the curse had been lifted, and with it the threats.

But there was something else I needed to do. You know how a photograph is when it first comes out of the developer? It's unstable. A stray shaft of light can wreck it. It has to be made permanent in another chemical, a fixer.

That's how I felt about my life at this stage. Like the

newly developed photograph, it had shape and beauty and composure, but there was something fragile about it. It needed that other process—fixing—so that it could endure the pressures of the world.

These were the thoughts that led me to ask Roy Davies to baptise us. Yes, us! Not just me, but all the family. We all shared a longing to be baptised publicly to let people see we wanted to serve God.

In my own case there was a second reason which only Roy and a few others knew about. Baptism would be a further barrier to Satan, and put me out of his reach for ever.

It was arranged that Roy would baptise us together at his church in Woodbury Road, Stourport, at the evening service on March 23rd in 1986—Palm Sunday.

We were all excited and a little bit nervous as we entered the church. We all knew the meaning of baptism. We'd read in the Bible how Jesus had been baptised, and the Holy Spirit had alighted on him like a dove. The first hymn was 'O Happy Day'. It was, too.

Only one thing went amiss during that memorable evening. It made it even more memorable. Something had gone wrong with the heater, and the water in the baptistry was freezing cold. But it didn't put us off. I kept looking at the water. I longed to get into it.

John was first, as head of the house. Then Liz followed. I hobbled in last. I was hobbling because my ankle was playing up. I was wearing a calliper and had to be helped down the steps.

Just before I entered the water, I gave my testimony. I said: 'I am being baptised because I want you to know Jesus Christ is the Lord of my life, and I want you to know I have been truly forgiven for things I used to get up to which I shouldn't have done.' I gave no details.

Roy and I had had a little chat earlier. Both of us knew there is a tendency for people who have been involved with the occult to try to keep one foot in the camp, so to speak. It had happened with me in a small way. Even though I had put the affairs of the coven behind me, I still kept in touch with one or two mediums.

In our talk, Roy had stressed that all these activities should cease. 'Cut all of those connections,' he had said. 'Satan is a master at getting in through the back door. Make sure the back door is shut.'

He led me into the water saying: 'On confession of your faith, I baptise you in the name of the Father, Son and Holy Spirit.'

I went under the water. Somehow it didn't seem cold. When I emerged, Roy's eyes met mine. Strangely, we uttered the words together: 'The back door's shut.'

And he added lovingly: 'Don't ever be tempted to turn the handle again.'

After changing out of our wet clothes, we joined the congregation for the rest of the service. The hymn was my favourite, and the words took on a new meaning for me.

> My shackles are gone, my spirit is free,
> Oh praise the Lord! He lifted me.
> My sins are forgiven, and now I am free.

Standing next to John and Liz, I experienced a warm secure feeling. I felt that God had got his arms around the family in such a way that Satan could never break us up.

I will always treasure the memory of my baptism, and the certificate I was given. The words from the Bible that accompany it are from Psalm 37 verse 17: 'For the power of the wicked will be broken, but the Lord upholds the righteous.'

That night I slept peacefully for the first time in years. There were no nightmares—and I haven't had one since.

16

Time to Tell

The new strength I felt after my baptism was not put into Christ's service immediately. But I began building upon it straight away. Every day I read my Bible, sometimes spending hours wrestling with the difficult bits until I had found a true understanding. And every day I prayed.

I was so happy with my new faith. It was as if somebody had placed a bowl of pure cool water in front of me. No matter how much I drank, I couldn't get enough.

People who knew me before noticed a dramatic change in my personality. My attitude was totally different. Now I was a nicer person, warmer, more loving, more tolerant—without that awful aggression I used to feel towards the world that got me into so much trouble.

Roy summed it up when he spoke to me after a prayer meeting in church one evening. 'I knew you had changed,' he said, 'when I saw you sitting in your seat weeping for somebody else instead of yourself.'

I wasn't consciously preparing myself to work for Christ. All my Bible study and prayer I was doing because I wanted to. There was no other purpose. It was simply that I loved God, and I wanted to be as good a follower as I could. The only way I could achieve it was by reading and praying and living.

I had no idea at this stage what the future would hold. But as the months went by and my faith became stronger, I began to realise that my awful past gave me the opportunity of performing a unique role. Having served Satan, I now wanted to serve God—using my inside knowledge of the enemy to help defeat him.

I now felt confident that I had, at last, shaken Satan off my back and put the curse that had blighted my life behind me. But I also felt something else. Previously I had been afraid people would find out about my evil past. Now I felt strong enough to tell them about it.

Don't get me wrong. I was, and am, ashamed of what I did. I don't talk about it with anything but shame. Nor do I revel in shocking people by disclosing the terrible sins which I committed, and which were done to me.

No, I talk about them for one reason only: as a warning to others that if they are foolish enough to dabble in witchcraft, or muck about with the occult, they could find themselves in the same deep trouble.

You have only to open the newspapers nowadays to see that Satan is as busy as ever. Tales of black magic are always in the headlines. Our courts are always hearing stories of satanic rituals. Our hospitals, especially mental hospitals, have many witchcraft victims among their patients.

Doctors, clergymen, social workers, probation officers, the police, child welfare officials, schoolteachers— all these and others whose work involves trying to find the underlying causes of crime, violence and other aberrations regularly come across evidence of the devil's work.

That is why, when I felt I had the strength, I decided to go public with my experiences. That is why I have written this book.

It is not a pretty tale. Parts are shocking and revolting. I have seen folk cringe and turn pale after listening to my story. I get no pleasure from telling it. But I shall continue to warn people, especially young people, at every opportunity about the threat witchcraft poses.

I know parts of my story are hard to believe. I realise there are some sceptics who will not accept that such things can happen behind the walls of pleasant suburban houses. There are some people, no doubt, who will accuse me of inventing the whole thing, or dreaming it all.

In a way I do not blame them. It is hard to believe that in modern times people meet to pay obeisance to Satan, and are prepared to go to the hideous lengths of sacrificing a child to please him.

Even some Christians refuse to believe in the forces of evil. I cannot think why. If they are prepared to accept there are forces for good, surely it is not inconceivable that there are forces pulling in the opposite direction.

The Bible tells us how it all began. Satan was an angel, created by God. He was an angel of light, a beautiful being, maybe the musician of heaven. Then when he tried to become more powerful than God, he got thrown out.

It is an aspect of spiritual life that lots of people don't like to face up to. Many Christians won't even talk about the devil. Yet surely the best way to be on your guard against a ruthless, cunning and determined enemy is to discuss him and his tactics, and prepare yourself for any attack. That's my view, but it's surprising how many people living in their own little world of perfect light do not share it.

My faith was becoming strong enough to go to war against Satan. Alas, my body wasn't. That old injury in my right ankle, which I got shinning down a drainpipe as I tried to make my escape from the hospital in Essex, was playing up again. I had twice had operations on it, but it had got worse. Now I needed elbow crutches to walk and there was even a wheelchair handy in case I should need that.

We went for a holiday in a caravan at the Mid-Wales Christian Holiday Centre at Cefn Lea Park near Newtown. Ray Bevan, the Welsh gospel singer, was there and Liz wanted to hear him. I went along grudgingly. The ankle was giving me a lot of pain, and I was not a very nice person.

The people who own the camp, the Morgans, are a lovely family. There was a prayer meeting on the Saturday night. I went to it but didn't really enjoy it. I went again on the Sunday morning. The pain in my ankle was becoming unbearable, and I asked the preacher to pray for some relief for me.

The prayer didn't work, and the pain was just as bad afterwards. But there was another meeting the next day, with Bob Gordon preaching. There was a girl in his team whose name I remember as Chrissie. After the meeting, she led a prayer for me.

I can only describe what happened as a miracle. I felt a surge going through me, like an electric current. I took my boots and callipers off and I found I could stand up without my crutches. Minutes later I was running around the field, yelling with joy like some crazy animal. For the first time in months I was free of pain.

On that holiday, we met some people from a Baptist church in Liverpool. I told them a little bit about my past, and they were fascinated. They gave me their name and address and invited me to go and stay with them, and tell the elders of their church about my experiences in witchcraft.

But it was a long time before I was able to accept their invitation. My ankle was better, but there were other more serious health problems. I had two strokes that autumn, and with the first I was rushed to hospital and spent three days in the intensive care unit. It wasn't a time for ministering to others. I had to get myself in shape first.

We went for another holiday to Cefn Lea. This time we had a real surprise. Sitting at the next table in the dining room was a man who kept looking at me.

He spoke to me after looking and listening for some time. 'I'm sure I recognise your voice,' he said.

My voice, as those who've heard it will testify, is pure East End. The man who had recognised it was Eldin Corsie, head of the Elim Pentecostal Church in Britain.

He used to hold prayer meetings at Kensington Temple in London, and he recognised me, or my voice anyway, from all those years ago when I used to stagger in, usually stoned on drugs.

When I told him my name, Audrey Wilbraham as it then was, he said: 'Yes, Audrey. I remember it. Frank Wilson told us about you. We used to pray for you regularly.'

I shook his hand and thanked him. 'The prayers worked,' I said. 'But they took an awfully long time. You and God have been very persistent!'

That year, we met our Liverpool friends again, and they repeated their plea for me to visit them. It was during this visit that, for the first time, I related my story to an audience—the full, unexpurgated version, leaving nothing out.

Somehow those people were so welcoming and interested I felt able to share with them the terrible things I had been involved in. We were in the home of one of the elders of Maghull Baptist Church. There were about eight or nine people there.

They listened attentively and without interruption to my story. Somehow it seemed natural that I should tell and they should listen. I even told them about the child sacrifice, the abuse of children, everything that had happened. If they were shocked, they didn't show it.

Afterwards they asked me to come to their church the following evening, which was Sunday, and tell their

congregation the same harrowing story. I agreed—but I
didn't tell the whole of it. The worst parts, like the rape
and sacrifice, I felt I couldn't describe at a normal service
in church. It would have been insensitive.

One of the men in that church was a member of the
Reachout Trust, and it was he who put me in touch with
the director, Doug Harris. The main purpose of the
Trust is to campaign against cults, such as the Moonies
and Jehovah's Witnesses, but they had decided at their
most recent conference that with the growing interest in
the occult, this was an area they should move into.

The problem was, Reachout had nobody on its books
with first-hand experience of the occult and its perils.
They wanted me—and I was now ready to take up the
challenge.

My assignment, as I saw it, was twofold. People, especially youngsters, had to be warned not to dabble. It
wasn't just witchcraft, although that obviously presented
the greatest danger. There were other things, some of
which appeared to be harmless games, which could ens-
nare victims by cultivating a fascination for occult practices.

Take ouija boards. They seem like a bit of innocent
fun. But I know of cases in which young boys and girls
have played these games as the first stage to becoming
witches. Tarot cards are much the same. They excite a
curiosity about the occult.

And the so-called games children play at Halloween
are just as insidious. I know carrying around a hollowed-
out pumpkin with a candle inside and putting on a mask
or tall hat seems a bit of harmless fun. But it's still a
celebration of a satanic festival.

Many leading churchmen have expressed their concern at these pursuits which are far from trivial. The
Reachout Trust felt that my experiences were so shocking that if I told people about them, even leaving out the

worst bits, it would give them such a fright they would steer clear of occult activities.

That was one part of my job. The other part was to teach the churches, and their leaders, how to fight witchcraft.

Most clergymen are quite ignorant of how to deal with it. By meeting me, a former witch, and hearing how I became involved and what it entailed, they would be better equipped to advise their own flocks of the dangers.

I set about my new duties with an energy and will which, with my health problems, surprised even me. One of the first tasks was to appear in a live television show on the subject of witchcraft. Considering I had never appeared on TV before, it was a daunting prospect. I'm sorry to say I made a hash of it.

It all came about when the Evangelical Alliance in London decided they had to do something about the burgeoning interest in the subject. Halloween was coming up, and they wanted to produce some literature warning young people that the sort of tricks they get up to at Halloween could be a first step to witchcraft.

Keith Ewing, an official of the Evangelical Alliance, had heard of me, and he wanted to include some of my background in this warning. But even he felt the account of the child being sacrificed was too shocking, so they left out that part of the story.

The Alliance put out a pamphlet, *Doorways to Danger*, that lists these seemingly innocent occult pastimes, such as the neighbourhood seance, or the astrologer's telephone helpline, which, as it says, 'could be entrances into a sinister world of evil and destruction'. And in it they included a very brief account of my tormented life as a witch, adding that it had been estimated that there were 30,000 active witches in the country.

The pamphlet was picked up by Tyne Tees Television, who decided to produce a Halloween programme on witchcraft. They invited me to go on as a former black witch, and join two white witches who had travelled over from Ireland.

I had only just got over my second stroke, and the family was apprehensive about how I'd stand up to it all—the long train journey to Newcastle upon Tyne and the tension of appearing on TV for the very first time, in a discussion that could be emotive and controversial.

We prayed together before I set out. On the train I found myself sitting with some students. They asked me why I was going to Newcastle, and, when I told them it was for a TV programme on witchcraft, one of them said: 'Ooh. You shouldn't get involved in that sort of thing. I'm told it can be dangerous.'

They were sweet girls, and I told them I had got myself involved—and what it had cost me. It was an opportunity to get my warning into a university. I have always tried to use every chance I can to spread my message.

But I missed my chance on the programme of getting my words of warning to the millions of viewers. I was very disappointed. After some mock witches danced around a cauldron, the Irish witches gave their defence of white witchcraft, and other people spoke.

The presenter said I had been involved in a black coven. I only said a few words—something like, 'I was drawn into a black coven and offered drugs.'

The presenter didn't seem to be very sympathetic towards my Christian outlook. She said: 'How do you know you were not just on a bad trip?'

I replied: 'A bad trip doesn't last five years.'

That was it—that was as much of my message as I was allowed to put across. The microphone never came back my way.

I was so upset, I'd had a good opportunity, and I felt I'd blown it. But it taught me a lesson which I never forgot in future television and radio interviews: Don't let go of the mike until you've had your say.

The next time I was on the box was in a BBC 2 *Open Space* programme. There had been an earlier programme on witchcraft, and there were protests that it was all pro with no anti. So the BBC put out an invitation to make a programme attacking witchcraft—and I was brought in to point out the dangers.

That was good. I was able to get my feelings over. And that was the start of a whole series of TV and radio appearances. Every time the phone rang it seemed I was being invited on to this chat show, or that documentary.

The Newcastle experience was a good lesson. I tried not to hog the microphone, but I jolly well made sure I held it for long enough to get my point across. I felt my warning was important, far more important than any defence of witchcraft, white or black, and I did my best to make sure nobody suppressed it.

About this time I found I had an unexpected ally. Several times in the House of Commons, a Member of Parliament had spoken of his worries at the growth of witchcraft. I hadn't heard of Geoffrey Dickens before. But a speech he made in April 1988 was well publicised and I decided to write to him.

What he had said was: 'Young people are in danger from the effects of witchcraft which is sweeping the country.' And he had asked for a debate saying many people who had been convicted of offences against children had been involved in witchcraft ceremonies.

My letter to him was a simple one. I told him how I had been raped at my initiation ceremony, and that I had seen a baby sacrificed to Satan. My letter was intended to encourage his campaign and to give him some confirmation that the dreadful things he suspected were actually happening. They had happened to me.

Shortly afterwards I was invited to appear on *Central Weekend*, a live television discussion programme broadcast in the Midlands. The subject was witchcraft. When I arrived at the Birmingham studios, I was delighted to find Geoffrey Dickens on the panel.

I introduced myself. He was intrigued to meet the writer of a letter containing such shocking disclosures. There and then he decided that what I had told him was too important to keep to ourselves.

'We must get this on the programme tonight so that the public realise what is going on,' he said. I was apprehensive. I didn't know my legal position. After all, I had witnessed a murder and never reported it. That must be a crime. Could I be arrested as an accessory after all these years?

Geoffrey insisted it was my duty to reveal what I knew. He was right. The time had come for me to tell the public the terrible things I had seen and participated in.

The producers were not expecting it. Nor was the studio audience. There were a number of witches on the programme—white and grey witches they called them-selves—who were there to say how harmless and inno-cent their religion is. They were not expecting it either.

First I told how the warlock had raped me at my initia-tion. Then Geoffrey turned towards me. He put the question slowly and deliberately.

'Audrey, to your knowledge, is child sacrifice going on?'

I replied: 'To my knowledge, yes.'

Just four words. But what a furore they caused! The witches were livid. They felt I had brought their beliefs into disrepute. One of them produced an effigy of Geof-frey Dickens and threatened to stick pins in it if he con-tinued his campaign. As we were leaving the studios, one said to me: 'We'll get you for this. Watch out.'

After all I had been through, a threat from a white witch meant nothing. If I was to be harmed, it would come from her black sisters. But now I felt strong enough to resist any attack.

A lot of people bundle all witches together under the one heading, witchcraft, but there is a difference between black and white witches.

White witches are followers of Wicca, the old pagan religion that predated Christ. They worship the elements—fire, water, earth and air. They are not followers of Satan. They don't even believe in him, but consider he is a concept dreamt up by the Christian church to frighten people.

Because of this, some people think they are harmless, and may even do good. They certainly do not set out to do evil, as black witches do.

As a Christian, I don't share the view that they are harmless. They mess about with magic to try to make sick people better, or to bring good fortune. Even if they don't do deliberate harm, their activities are opposed to Christian teachings because they worship false gods.

Black witches, who meet in covens under a warlock, not only worship Satan, but they try to invoke him to bestow his powers upon them to do evil. They delight in everything that is unlawful under the Christian code. They happily abase themselves and abuse others to try to please Satan.

There is another larger group who also worship Satan in satanic temples. These people are not so secretive as members of a black coven, whose numbers are strictly limited to thirteen witches, usually all female, and the warlock, a male.

There is not so much secrecy at these satanic temples, and they do not involve themselves in rituals quite so horrifying as I witnessed in the coven—the sacrifice of a child.

In spite of the fact that there are varying degrees of evil in witchcraft, I am opposed to all of them. It is very easy to progress from white witchcraft to black witchcraft once the curiosity is aroused.

My warning to the people I meet, especially young people, is to steer clear of all witchcraft, and everything else to do with the occult.

As well as getting that warning across to television viewers, I was speaking to church and school groups. The next opportunity Reachout gave me was to address a crowd of people, drawn from the public at large, who had gathered because they were interested in the subject.

That crowd must have included witches, tarot card readers, horoscope tellers, the lot. Altogether there were 400 of them in a theatre at Colwyn Bay in North Wales.

Maureen Davies, the Reachout representative in North Wales, had organised the meeting. I was a bit scared because Maureen had received some phone calls from witches before the meeting saying they were going to come in force and grab the microphone.

Just before it was due to start, I heard someone rattling the backdoor. I had visions of witches pouring in and wrecking the meeting. It was quite nerve-racking, especially in an area which is reputed to have a lot of occult activity.

Maureen and Doug Harris joined me in a prayer before we opened the doors and admitted the crowd. A group of witches managed to bag the front seats. But they didn't give me any bother at all. They sat quietly and listened as I sketched out my life story, emphasising how the love of God had triumphed after years of torment as I tried to shake off the curse the coven put on me.

I didn't tell them about the rape, or the pornography, or the murder of that baby. You have to judge who to tell these things to, and when to tell them. That night I felt it would be wrong. I was able to get my message across with its warning without going into the horror aspects of my past.

One young girl came forward to say she had noises in her head, and had been to a spiritualist church where she had been told to nurture those voices. She said she wanted to become a Christian, and yet keep those powers.

I was firm with her and said: 'Well, you can't.'

She went away, apparently one of my failures. But plenty of others came forward to make a commitment to Christ.

I have another outstanding memory of that trip to Wales. Earlier Maureen had arranged for me to meet a party of church workers and youth leaders in Rhyl. There were about thirty people at this meeting. And on this occasion my judgement was that they should hear the whole of my story.

They listened with interest and understanding. Their main concern appeared to be the desperate difficulty I had getting away from the coven and eventually escaping the curse. For the professionals in the ministry, that, I suppose, is the main problem—helping people who have embraced Satan, but who now want to put him behind them.

As well as speaking up and down the country on their behalf, Reachout have found another way of getting my warning to vulnerable young people. They have produced a video recording of me telling my story which they lend to anyone who wants to see it.

All of this exposure on TV, in the press, at meetings, in churches, produces an enormous response. All sorts of people track down my telephone number, or send me letters—people who are victims of Satan, or know victims, and think I can help.

It's a serious business, but sometimes it's touched with humour. I can't help chuckling at the call I received from a lady doctor who asked me for help on one of her cases—a woman who claimed Satan was controlling her mind.

The doctor came to see me at my home. She was, it turned out, a psychiatrist. After all the psychiatrists I'd seen in my years under the curse when I was in and out of mental hospitals, here I was giving advice to one on how she could cure her patient. Ironical was hardly the word!

The doctor said: 'I'm so glad I came to see you. It means I can now believe what my patient is telling me. Like you, she says she has seen a baby sacrificed. I didn't believe her at first. But having heard your story, now I do.'

17

The Battle Continues

Every year I travel hundreds of miles around the country doing battle with Satan. My work with the Reachout Trust brings me into contact with hundreds of young people. It enables me to cheat Satan of many potential victims. This gives me great joy.

But it is also tinged with sadness. On my travels, I so often meet people who are trying to escape from the evils of witchcraft after Satan has wrecked their lives.

I suppose I was one of the fortunate ones. It took a long, long time but eventually I made it. With lots of help from many good people, and the blessing of God, I managed to put Satan behind me.

But many of these people I meet are not so fortunate. Their lives are still damned, as mine was for all those years when I lived in the shadow of the devil's curse.

We live in a sceptical society. As there are large numbers of people who refuse to believe in the good works of God, so there are equally large numbers who disregard the evil powers of Satan. That is the saddest aspect of all. In my case I eventually met people who believed my story and helped me. But many of today's victims are not believed, and there is nobody to help them.

More recently I took part in a Roger Cook TV investigation into the links between witchcraft and child abuse—links which have been proved to be very strong, as my own story illustrates.

At a church near Blackburn in Lancashire, not far from Pendle Hill which was historically notorious for its witches, families involved in the Cook programme gathered to pray.

I have heard and seen some terrible things in my career as a witch, and later as a counsellor against witchcraft. But nothing could be so pathetic as the stories I heard from those families whose lives had been ruined by Satan. They filled my eyes with tears.

One poor woman from Humberside could hardly speak because of her grief. Her nine-year-old son had been taken by his father into a coven, fed magic mushrooms to drug him and then abused, not only by his father but by four other perverts.

When social workers first heard this story, they refused to believe it. They said the boy had made it up. Yet subsequently he identified one of the men who had abused him. The man was charged and put on probation.

That woman is now divorced, but her life when I last heard of her was beset with problems. And who was behind them all? Satan.

I met a young mother from Nottingham who was there with her baby. This woman came from a family of Satan-worshippers, and had been abused since she was a youngster by her grandfather. She was so upset by the memories of it all that she sobbed as she spoke to me.

There was another young mother from London with three children, one of them a baby. The two older children had been taken to a coven by their father. Both of them, a boy and a girl, were abused by a number of satanists when they were just two and four years old.

All of these people cried for help. But their cries went unheard. The police found their stories incredible, and took no action. Social workers thought the children were fantasising, and took no action. Nobody took action.

Nobody believed them.

Why, oh why won't the authorities believe these horror stories? It's as if there is some official plan to refuse to acknowledge the existence of Satan. Yet the child abuse seems to be on the increase everywhere.

It must give Satan great pleasure to see these evils perpetrated, and the torment go on and on endlessly because our stubborn society refuses to acknowledge how real his powers are.

I often weep when I think about the utter hopelessness of these young lives inextricably caught up in Satan's web of evil. I know what they are going through. I've been there—and it was the fear that my story wouldn't be believed that kept me there.

The rescue work I undertake is much more difficult than my preventive role. There are young people who come to me seeking help—but when I try to give it they suddenly rebel and decide to go back to their old ways.

With my past, I can understand this. Satan, once he's got you, doesn't want to let go. Look at the struggle I had. For nearly twenty years people were trying to help me—but I kept going back to Satan.

There is only one answer—caring and persistent counselling and prayer. Alas, there are few people who can give it. Even clergymen lack the necessary skills and experience. A few have them—but apparently precious few.

I have had no training in dealing with problems of the mind, other than as a nurse in my younger days. But what I have got is probably much more valuable. Because I've been there and done it, I can recognise genuine cases where Satan has taken over the minds of victims. And I believe I am in a strong position, with God's help, to assist them.

There are many people in different parts of the country whom I have helped to get away from the influence of covens. Some, no doubt, will go back if they haven't done so already. But I'm persistent, and I shall continue trying to help them no matter how much energy and prayer it takes.

There is a girl from Sussex whom I'll call Denise. She was in and out of trouble for years, and she did some terrible things. She was the daughter of a witch, and her father was high priest in a coven. She had been brought up in witchcraft. She was raped in her teens and had been sexually abused by her father all her life.

Denise was twenty when I got to know her, a beautiful looking girl. But she had no concept of ordinary morals. She deliberately set out to seduce some of the men in a church she joined just to be disruptive and create family problems.

She kept coming and going. Sometimes she said she wanted out—other times she was quite happy to go along with the coven. But I continued trying to help her, and I'll always pray for her. She'll need those prayers for a long time yet.

Another of my cases—I'll call her Rose—lived in the West Midlands, a part of the country that seems to buzz with witchcraft activity. Rose was taken into a coven by her parents, and made pregnant four times by a warlock so that the babies could be sacrificed to Satan.

Each time she had an abortion, members of the coven actually ate the foetus. There are no limits to the depravity of witches in their perverse desire to please their evil master.

When she was in her early teens, Rose was taken into care by a local authority. But then she was actually handed back to the parents who did these awful things to her. Nobody would believe her when in her faltering voice she tried to tell what was happening.

Now I'm glad to say she has broken away from them. I, along with some Christian helpers, have tried to make sure she stays away. But she has two younger sisters who were still at home and the same thing was happening to them.

To help people like Denise and Rose, I have set up a network of advisers spread all over the country. In time I hope that whenever I get a call for help, wherever it comes from, there will be somebody nearby who can respond immediately and know just how to handle the situation.

None of this work would be possible without God's help. It is prayer, pure concentrated prayer, and our love for Christ that keeps me, and others like me, ever ready to step in to do battle with Satan, whatever strokes he tries to pull.

Witchcraft is a growing religion, there's no doubt about that. The Evangelical Alliance estimates there are 30,000 practising witches in Britain today. I have heard far higher estimates putting the number at a frightening 200,000.

I don't suppose anyone can be sure. Witches are not the sort of people who step forward for a census to be taken. But in almost every part of the country I have heard reports from devout Christians who say they suspect, or can detect, an alarming growth in occult practices. There are active covens in every town and city.

There are magazines on open sale which advertise covens looking for recruits, and recruits looking for covens. Anyone who takes the trouble to study these advertisements will observe more people are looking for covens which take the LH path (the left hand path to black witchcraft) than the RH path (the right hand path to white witchcraft).

The occult fairs and psychic festivals which take place up and down the country draw huge attendances. Ask at any library and they will tell you of the interest in books on witchcraft and the occult. It's not surprising that these are the books most frequently stolen, as well as borrowed, from libraries.

All sorts of people, from all walks of life, are drawn into witchcraft. Satan is not selective. But he does seem to favour young recruits. Why should this be? Why does witchcraft hold such a fascination for so many young people?

I find this aspect particularly worrying, especially when I think about my own case. It was the urge for power, and for the company of well-to-do people, that attracted me. Satan, through the coven, promised me wealth and power. I didn't get either, but I'm not surprised, knowing that he is the great deceiver.

Today's youngsters are concerned about lots of things in the world. They are worried about the bomb, about the environment, about what is being put into our food and spread upon our land. They think about their future, and the future of their families.

I hate to say it, but the church, which should have provided answers for them, hasn't always done so. The church has fallen down badly on the job of attracting young people. Perhaps if it had done a better job, youngsters who have followed Satan would have turned to God instead.

Satan's recruiting agents are out and about and as busy as ever. I even heard of one case where a school in North Wales had set up a help-line for pupils who found themselves in difficulties with occult situations. But giving advice at the other end of the line to help these children sort out their problems was a witch. The leader of the local coven, with the help of her sixteen-year-old daughter who was a pupil at the school, had gained access to all these children with difficult emotional problems on their minds. A happy hunting ground for Satan.

It would be nice if a law could be passed banning witchcraft. But that cannot happen. In this country we are proud of our religious freedom, and witchcraft claims to be a religion. The law does not differentiate between black and white witches. Worshipping Satan is not, in itself, a crime, even though some of his followers commit the most ghastly and despicable offences.

No, there's no political or legal solution to the problem. The only way to fight it is on a spiritual level. God will always defeat Satan. If people believe fervently in God and commit themselves to Christ, Satan won't be able to get near them.

I shall go on fighting Satan. For a large part of my life, he ruled me. As his dancing partner for many years, I know how powerful he is. I know how powerful his disciples are.

But I've seen him beaten—and now I want to show others how to beat him. If we are on our guard, if the stronger of us look after the weaker, if we don't dismiss Satan and recognise how powerful and dangerous he can be, we can beat him. With God's help.

Every night and often during the day, I pray to God to give me strength to continue my battle. Satan did his utmost to ruin my life. I'm determined to do all I can to stop him ruining the lives of others.

Paganism And The Occult

by Kevin Logan

Mediums, ouija boards, white witches, chaos magic, Satanism, the paranormal...

What are we to make of the current upsurge in pagan beliefs and occult rituals? Are they all basically the same, or are some good and the others bad? And are there mysterious powers which modern science has failed to classify which can be used for either good or evil?

Kevin Logan is Vicar of St John's Great Harwood, in Lancashire, and has helped many break free from occult practices. He calls on other Christians to reach out to those who are disillusioned with the unsatisfying rewards of pagnism and the destructive influence of the occult.

Acknowledged expert on the occult and paranormal phenomena John Allan writes: 'Kevin Logan's insistence that Christians can minister to witches and others involved in the occult is much needed if we are to make any impact upon this growing group.'

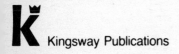

Kingsway Publications

The Occult And Young People

by Roger Ellis

Witches, horoscopes, ouija boards, reincarnation...

Day by day our senses are bombarded by occult propaganda; books on spiritism, newspaper reports on the paranormal, horoscopes on the radio, while New Age is all the rage.

This book warns of the dangers of dabbling with forces beyond our control. It also shows a way out for those who have been spiritually and emotionally wounded by demonic powers.

Roger Ellis lays the groundwork for a biblical understanding of the occult and the supernatural, as well as showing us how to take a positive Christian stand in spiritual warfare.

Roger Ellis is based at the Revelation Christian Fellowship in Sussex. He is a member of the Pioneer Team, and has been a regular speaker at Spring Harvest.

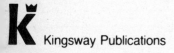

Kingsway Publications

A Brilliant Deception

by Chris Kline

Where do you go when you're young and looking for love?

Living life in the fast lane, Chris enjoyed the drugs and rock scene of the Hollywood jet set. At least, she told herself she did.

But when the glamour lost its shine, Chris was drawn to the supernatural. One night she had a 'visitor', someone—or something—that could tell her things no human would know.

Was this the answer to her search for love and truth? Chris Kline's story reveals the power of occult forces, and the spiritual warfare that is taking place in the world today.

'Are Satan and God real? Do they influence? The answer is in these pages.'

Frank Barron
Hollywood TV programme creator
twice editor of Billboard Publications

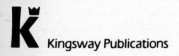

Kingsway Publications